EXEMPLARS OF TRUTH

EXEMPLARS OF TRUTH

KEITH LEHRER

OXFORD
UNIVERSITY PRESS

OXFORD
UNIVERSITY PRESS

Oxford University Press is a department of the University of Oxford. It furthers
the University's objective of excellence in research, scholarship, and education
by publishing worldwide. Oxford is a registered trade mark of Oxford University
Press in the UK and certain other countries.

Published in the United States of America by Oxford University Press
198 Madison Avenue, New York, NY 10016, United States of America.

CIP data is on file at the Library of Congress
ISBN 978-0-19-088427-7

9 8 7 6 5 4 3 2 1

Printed by Sheridan Books, Inc., United States of America

CONTENTS

ACKNOWLEDGMENTS

The philosophers to whom I refer most often in the text are Wilfrid Sellars, Roderick Chisholm, Edmund Gettier, Willard Van Orman Quine, Nelson Goodman, Wittgenstein, David Hume, and especially Thomas Reid. However, Ernest Sosa, Peter Klein, Alvin Goldman, Fred Dretske, Linda Zagzebski, and Jerry Fodor have all influenced and provoked, sometimes with opposition, what I have written. Then there are colleagues here to acknowledge, especially Mark Timmons, who organized a reading group on the text and offered invaluable advice. My colleagues in Tucson who were always ready to discuss my work on the project include Chris Maloney, Terry Horgan, Jenann Ismael, Juan Comesaña, Joseph Tolliver, Stewart Cohen, and my wife and collaborator, Adrienne Lehrer. Of special importance to the completion and critical evaluation of the manuscript are my graduate students, most especially Weston Siscoe, who often drove the project and edited it, Josh Cangelosi, and Phoebe Chan. I also wish to thank Cherie Braden, who provided invaluable comments. Leopold Stubenberg, Marian David, Martina Fürst, and Guido Melchior amended and hopefully improved the project with their constructive and critical insights. These latter connections would not have occurred without the invitation of the late Rudolf Haller to Graz, Austria, and his invaluable personal and philosophical support. I owe him a great debt of gratitude.

There are other acknowledgments extending back to the publication of (Bogdan, 1980) of essays about my work. It is with great pleasure that I acknowledge the many articles written about my work in epistemology that have influenced my thought and work. I am grateful to Radu Bogdan for editing a book about my philosophy so early in my career that contained challenging articles by George S. Pappas, A. K. Bjerring and C. A. Hooker, and Mark Pastin. I also wish to acknowledge the excellent articles about my epistemology and that of L. Bonjour in Bender (1989) written by Paul K. Moser, G. J. Mattey, Wayne Davis, John W. Bender, Richard Feldman, Philip L. Peterson, and Bruce Russell. After this book, a book edited by Brandl, Gombocz, and Piller (1991) based on a volume of *Grazer Philosophische Studien* about my philosophy contained important articles written by Fred Dretske, Christian Piller, Alfred Schramm, Marian David, Mylan Engel, Daniel Schulthess, and Elvio Baccarini. I should also acknowledge many excellent essays about my epistemology in Olsson (2003) written by Erik J. Olsson, Ernest Sosa, John Greco, Jonathan L. Kvanvig, Todd Stewart, Volker Halbach, Glenn Ross, Charles B. Cross, Wolfgang Spohn, Carl G. Wagner, James Van Cleve, G. J. Mattey, Richard N. Manning, Hans Rott, Gordian Haas, Jacob Rosenthal, John W. Bender, Peter Klein, and David A. Truncellito. Most recently, I wish to acknowledge essays about my epistemology in a volume of *Philosophical Studies*, edited by Martina Fürst and Guido Melchior (2012), that contained articles that have influenced the present work by Marian David, Pascal Engel, Hannah Tierney and Nicholas D. Smith, Guido Melchior, Nenad Miščević, Kristin Borgwald, Anita Konzelmann Ziv, Danilo Šuster, Johann C. Marek, Leopold Stubenberg, Martina Fürst, and Joseph T. Tolliver. I have replied to all of these essays and articles in the books and volumes that contained them, but I did not stop reflecting on them, nor was their influence lost after I replied. There are many other articles in addition to these written about my work, but discussion of all of them would be a very lengthy tome. I wish instead to provide a succinct statement of where half a century of reflecting on epistemology has led me. It is what I have to offer at this late point in my life. I do not say that I am ready to quit, and, indeed, I hope that the publication of this volume will lead to further philosophical reflection, disputation, and discussion. It has been both a pleasure and honor to participate in the discussion about knowledge with those cited here and others who have taken the time to write about my work. I thank them with gratitude and a sense of humility that they have so honored me with their attention to what I have written.

Finally, I gratefully acknowledge permission granted to reprint, waiving all fees, the substance of Chapter 5 by Grant Osborn of Notre Dame University, which was originally printed by the University of Notre Dame Press in *Forms of Truth and the Unity of Knowledge*, edited by Vittorio Hösle (2014), resulting from a conference hosted by the Notre Dame Institute for Advanced Study. I also gratefully acknowledge the permission to reprint the substance of Chapter 2, published by the Taylor and

Francis Group in *Inquiry: An Interdisciplinary Journal of Philosophy* in accordance with the contractual agreement that the author may republish said article in any work of which he is the sole author waiving all fees. Some material in Chapter 2 is taken from my paper "Defeasible Reasoning and Representation: The Lesson of Gettier" in a forthcoming book from Oxford University Press, *Explaining Knowledge: New Essays on the Gettier Problem,* and is included in the present volume with the permission of Oxford University Press.

Last but not least, I wish to acknowledge the remarkable advice and support of Peter Ohlin of Oxford University Press.

INTRODUCTION

AS I LOOKED AT MY WORK over more than half a century, it fit together in a systematic way that surprised me and motivated the present manuscript. I have written about knowledge, self-trust, consciousness, and autonomy. This resulted in books and volumes of journals collecting deeply insightful articles about what I had written—Bogdan (1980); Bender (1989); Brandl, Gombocz, and Pillar (1991); Olsson (2003), and Fürst and Melchior (2012). How could all that fit together into one system? The answer is this volume, but here is the short story. What unifies my thought is the theme of the critical evaluation of the initial states of desire, belief, and conception. Social scientists provide us with accounts of how these states arise and their defects. What we desire, believe, and conceive is often irrational. So what is a philosopher to contribute? A theory of how evaluation of these states takes us to a higher plane of what it is reasonable for an autonomous and trustworthy agent to prefer, to accept, and to think. It is natural for the social scientist to look for regularities, universal or stochastic principles, that govern our thought and action. Finding such laws is the invaluable game of science. But they, like the rest of us, confront the question of the reasonableness, justification, and defensibility of what they study. The answer to the question is creative evaluation and innovative reconfiguration provoked by thought and experience. Science, art, and practice challenge us to evaluate and reconsider what we desire, what we believe, and how we represent the world, ourselves in the world, and the world in ourselves. We must make ourselves worthy of our trust and the trust of others in our defensible quest for truth and value. We embody that defensible system of truth, value, theory, and practice. Here is my system.

DEFENSIBLE KNOWLEDGE

AND EXEMPLARS

REPRESENTATION

INTRODUCTION

After writing a number of books on knowledge, the question arises—Why another? The answer is brief. There was a history of epistemology aimed at finding certain and infallible statements as a foundation, a tradition advanced by Schlick (1979) and Ayer (1940) among others in the 20th century. The effort failed. The reason is that all description is fallible and because we are fallible in our use of language. That led to a view that knowledge must result from the relation to a background system of description, which, though fallible, is the basis for the defense and justification of knowledge claims. This was a view defended in various forms by Neurath (2008), who opposed the foundational theory, and in unique ways by Quine (1960), Sellars (1963a), and myself. I have called it (Lehrer, 1974) the *coherence theory*. However, all of the authors were left with the problem of explaining the special role of experience in the background system. This book offers a solution to the problem of the role of experience. The solution presented in this book is that reflection on experience converts the experience itself into an exemplar, something like a sample that becomes a vehicle of representation. The special role of the exemplar of experience is to be at the same time the term of representation and the object represented. The exemplar represents itself and exhibits something about evidence and truth concerning experience that, as Wittgenstein ([1922] 1999) noted, cannot be fully described but can only be shown. Exemplar representation is the missing component that links a background system to truth about the world.

AN OVERVIEW

Good philosophy should contain something old, something new, something borrowed, and something true. In *Knowledge* (Lehrer, 1974), I defended a coherence theory of knowledge based on a theory of justification construed as the capacity to meet objections to the knowledge claim in terms of global features of a background system of belief. Here, I maintain the view that knowledge is the capacity to meet objections in terms of a background system. That is something old. Something new is that I now construe the capacity as a *local defense* of the target claim, and I construe the system as an *evaluation system* of claims that are positively evaluated and autonomously accepted combined with preferences over states of acceptance and reasonings involving such states. Most critically, I amend my view to include something borrowed from Hume (1888) about sensory experience. That is a theory of the relation of the background system to exemplar representations of experience. Using experience as a vehicle of representation has a reflexive truth security, though the operation of representation is fallible, as are all the operations of the mind.

Exemplar representation provides a truth security from the process of reflexive exemplarization of sensations. However, that security is consistent with my earlier claim (Lehrer, 1974) that beliefs about the character of sensations and thoughts are corrigible as a result of the influence of the background system. I may know from exemplarization what a sensation is like, but, at the same time, form a false belief about the sensation. My earlier example (Lehrer, 1974) was a person informed by a respected physician that itches are mild pains. The person believes, accepts, that he has a pain when he itches, and as a result the belief is false. Taking an aspirin will not relieve the itch. Even if the person knows what the itch is like from exemplarization, he may misidentify it as a pain from the influence of background beliefs and the possibility of error. The process of exemplarizing may itself be cognitively distorted by background beliefs, and even where it is effective and not distorted, that is only a contingent fact. The truth security of exemplar representation does not supply the logical impossibility of error. The logical possibility of error is ubiquitous and exhibits how we are fallible. Nevertheless, exemplar representation can provide evidence and defense for what we accept.

Finally, I argue that we have an exemplar representation of the evidence of truth and of truth itself. This may leave you wondering whether I have abandoned coherentism for foundationalism. The answer is explained in the last chapter. I seek to offer you something both new and true.

GLOBAL COHERENCE VERSUS LOCAL DEFENSE

I called my theory a coherence theory because justification and defense of a knowledge claim's target content depends on a relation to a background system, but it is better named as a *defensibility theory of knowledge* as Kim suggested in his doctoral dissertation at the University of Arizona (1992). The features of the background system that enable the subject to meet objections to the target content are usually *local* features of the system relevant for the *specific defense* of that content rather than global features of the system. Defense of the target content directs the background system toward what is relevant for the defense of that content and meeting those objections. The theory of defensible knowledge has itself been modified to meet objections, as I shall explain below. Central to the modification is a theory of representation to explain how the background system is connected with truth by the evidence of experience. A theory of exemplarized experience explains the connection. I turn now to a brief narrative of my efforts to articulate a satisfactory coherence theory of defensible knowledge.

Objections arose to what I argued, and the justification of my epistemology required that I answer the objections my views elicited. This resulted in the publication of later books, *Theory of Knowledge* (1990) and *Theory of Knowledge,* 2nd edition (2000b), as well as a sequence of published papers. There were changes of details, and details are important, but I want to make it clear what central idea motivates the theory I have been articulating over half a century. It is a simple idea motivated by a line in Sellars (1963a). He remarked that reliable belief formation was not sufficient for knowledge because it neglected the role of what I called the *justification game* in human knowledge. His point was that a true belief could arise in a reliable manner though the subject is unable to justify the acceptance of the belief. Belief, not even reliably formed belief, is enough for knowledge. One must have adequate evidence and be able to articulate it to succeed in the justification game of knowledge.

THE JUSTIFICATION GAME AND KNOWLEDGE

That led me to ask what success in the justification game requires. My answer was that success requires that one be able to meet objections to the target content of knowledge. One may know things without actively engaging in the justification game, without actually reflecting on objections and answering them. But one must have the capacity to succeed in the justification game. What gives one that capacity to defend the target content of knowledge? A background system supplies the capacity to evaluate the reasonableness of objections and replies to them. I first thought of a background system as simply a system of beliefs. However, not all beliefs are reasonable, and the evaluation of beliefs by a subject will lead him to reasonably accept some and reject others. Only the ones that he accepts provide the capacity for defending the target content, and so it is an acceptance system that is the basis of success in the justification game. Yet there was clearly more than the appeal to acceptance in the justification game. Reasoning in terms of those acceptances would be required to evaluate and meet objections. Such reasonings must be part of the background system that yields the capacity to consider and meet objections in a reasonable manner. What one accepts and how one reasons in terms of what one accepts may not enter explicitly into conscious reflection of the subject but may remain ready as moves in the justification game. They are like the expert moves in a game of chess ready to become part of the justification game when opposition arises. Finally, in addition to what one accepts, there are preferences for accepting one thing over another not previously considered that will result in the choice to accept one thing over another when confronted with the choice. Common sense views are ones a person may prefer accepting to fanciful skeptical hypotheses about demons or brain manipulators one has never considered. Thus, the background system consists of what a person accepts, what he prefers to accept, and how he reasons with what he accepts. I have called it his *evaluation system.*

There is, however, an implicit assumption in the claim that the background evaluation system of acceptances, preferences over acceptances, and reasonings with acceptances enables the subject to *justify* the target content. The person must be reasonable in what he accepts, what he prefers to accept, and how he reasons. For if the person is not reasonable, the justification in terms of his system is counterfeit. But where is the reasoning that the person is reasonable? The answer I gave in *Self-Trust* (1997) is derived from my book on Reid (1989) and elaborated in Chapter 5. In presenting a set of first principles of the mind, Reid includes a principle that he says has a priority in the order of evidence over all the others, a principle I have called the *First First Principle*, to wit, that our faculties by which we distinguish truth from error are not fallacious but, instead, are trustworthy. I propose a modification of the principle, which does not contain a reference to faculties. Put in the first person, it is the normative principle that I am trustworthy in what I accept to satisfy the norms of reason, most notably, to obtain truth and avoid error. The principle supports what I accept, and, at the same time, it is supported by what I accept. It is not a bootstrap pulling itself up. It depends for support on other things that I accept. I have suggested the metaphor of a keystone in an arch that supports the position of the other stones in the arch at the same time that they support it. Reid suggested the analogy of light, which reveals itself as it reveals the objects it illuminates. However, the important feature of the principle of trustworthiness is the epistemic notion of being *worthy* of trust for oneself and others in what one accepts to satisfy the norms of reason. To be worthy of trust in what one accepts requires autonomy in what one accepts as well as what one prefers to accept or how one reasons. A high frequency of a person accepting what is true over what is false is not sufficient for trustworthiness because the frequency of success might not conform to autonomously following the norms of reason in a way that makes him worthy of trust for himself and others.

It is crucial to an understanding of my account of the trustworthiness of a person that it depends on a social factor of having the capacity to meet objections of others even if the person is not actually confronted with those objections. The capacity may be reflected in the preferences of the person for accepting replies to objections that have not been raised. Preferences over alternatives concerning what one accepts, like other preferences, may be preferences over alternatives not yet considered. Some alternative hypotheses of deception, like evil demon or brain in vat alternatives, may be ones a person prefers not to accept in a choice between accepting them and other hypotheses, such as those of perception of the external world, even though the hypotheses of deception have not been considered. So success frequency in reaching truth is not sufficient for being trustworthy in what one accepts, even if obtaining truth and avoiding error are the primary goals of reason. For being trustworthy requires the capacity to defend what one accepts against objections in accord with the norms of reason. This may be more obvious if the issue is formulated in terms of reasonableness rather than trustworthiness. The success frequency of a person in reaching truth is not enough to entail that he is reasonable in what he accepts when he lacks a defense of the way that he proceeds. A person is reasonable in what he accepts when he has a reason for thinking he is reasonable to proceed in the way he does. That requires the principle of trustworthiness. It requires both the acceptance of the principle and the truth of the principle. The reasoning from the principle of trustworthiness to the reasonableness of what one accepts is sound only if the premises of it are true. The principle of trustworthiness is a keystone premise in the reasoning.

If a person knows that p, then it must be true that p. But beyond that connection with truth, there is the question of the relationship of the connection between justification and truth. Justification, what I have called *personal justification*, depends on the capacity of the evaluation system of a person to enable the person to meet objections to the target content of alleged knowledge. However, the evaluation system at a given time must supply that capacity in defense of the target knowledge claim—at the time knowledge is claimed—to yield the personal justification required for knowledge at that time. This is contrary to the claim of Leite (2004) that thought and reasoning arising from the later acquisition of a capacity may suffice for defense of an earlier knowledge claim. It is necessary and sufficient for personal justification at a given time required for knowledge at that time that all objections to the target content can be met, that is, beaten or dismissed by the acceptances and preferences over acceptances and reasonings already contained in the evaluation system *at the given time*. Something is an objection *o* to the target content *c* just in case *c* is less reasonable for the subject *S* to accept if the objection is true than if it is false. If all objections can be beaten or dismissed in terms of the evaluation system of the subject, then the subject can defend the target content, and this personally justifies the subject in accepting it. An objection is beaten just in case it is more reasonable for the person to accept the target than to accept the objection. An objection can be dismissed, what I previously call *neutralized*, just in case something the subject prefers to accept has the result that, when added as a comment on the objection, the elaborated conjunction is not an objection to the target. The objection is dismissed because the target content is no less reasonable if the conjunction is true than if the objection is true.

However, these notions of beating and dismissing objections on the evaluation system depend on the evaluation system, yielding the result that one thing is more or less *reasonable* for S to accept. Personal justification depends on the reasonableness of the evaluation system of the subject and, therefore, on the trustworthiness and reasonableness of the subject. The subject must be reasonable in what he accepts in the background system to yield personal justification. A person who fails to be reasonable, fails to be trustworthy in satisfying the goals of reason, is not personally justified in what he accepts even if he accepts that he is reasonable and trustworthy. If the principle of trustworthiness is false, the light of evidence is extinguished, and the arch of evidence collapses. Not everything a person accepts need be true for the evaluation system to yield personal justification, but truth of the principle of trustworthiness is essential for the reasonableness of the system.

THE TRUTH CONNECTION UNDER FALLIBILITY: SOLVING THE GETTIER PROBLEM

To complete our account of knowledge, we require a deeper connection with truth. The reason, already implicit, is that we are fallible in what we accept and we may go awry in our pursuit and be deceived in ways we do not detect. The most notable consequence in the literature, the Gettier problem (1963), has led to a complex literature including my article (Lehrer, 1980). The problem can be simply formulated once our fallibility is acknowledged. For if we are fallible in what we accept, then we may be justified, on my account personally justified, in accepting something that is false. Gettier noted that we may deduce a truth from something false, even from something false we are justified in accepting. The justification will be transferred by deduction from a false but justified premise to a true conclusion. But the true conclusion, deduced from a false premise, is not knowledge because acceptance of it is based on a false premise. Moreover, once our fallibility is acknowledged, the dependence of accepting something true on the justified acceptance of something false need not proceed by valid deduction, though that is a compelling example. Errors in how we represent the world arising from perception, for example, may influence what we accept without proceeding from deduction from such representation.

Chisholm (1966) extended the problem that Gettier raised to false representation arising from perception. For Chisholm noted that a problem similar to those that Gettier had raised might result in the case of perception without any obvious use of reasoning. The example from Chisholm was a person who sees an object in the distance in a field that he takes to be a sheep. So he believes he sees sheep in the field, and being an experienced sheepherder who knows what a sheep looks like, is justified in this belief. Moreover, next to the rock stands a sheep, which he also sees, though he does not take that object, which is in fact a sheep, to be a sheep. However trustworthy our sheepherder is at discerning a sheep from a rock, he is mistaken in this instance, for what he takes to be a sheep is a rock. There is a sheep in the field that he sees, but he does not take that object to be a sheep, because he ignores it. So our sheepherder has a justified true belief that he sees a sheep in the field, even though what he takes to be a sheep is not a sheep. He sees a sheep in the field, but he does not take that object to be a sheep. So in this example, though no reasoning seems to be involved, a person, our sheepherder, has a justified true belief that he sees a sheep in the field, but the belief is not knowledge. The reason that it fails to be knowledge is that it depends on a mistake of taking something to be a sheep that is not a sheep. The belief of the sheepherder rests on that error. So the problem has deepened from one about fallible reasoning to one about fallible representation. There is an error in the representation of the sheepherder that leads us to deny that he knows.

The Gettier problem was not just a technical problem for the analysis of knowledge as justified true belief. It was a problem for any account of knowledge that acknowledges our fallibility and the defeasibility of justification resulting therefrom. Now we have the core and depth of the problem before us. We must acknowledge that a belief that is true may also be as well justified as we as we can attain while depending on some error as I argued earlier (Lehrer, 1974) followed by Zagzebski (1994). Since it depends on error, the truth of the belief depends on something false. The problem now becomes one of explaining how justification, or if you prefer, evidence, can lead to knowledge from representation or reasoning when it not does not depend on anything false. The solution to the problem is not some simple technical fix of the definition of knowledge as justified true belief. The solution requires an account of the way in which justification does not depend on error while conceding that justification rests on our fallibility and allows for error.

Epistemology acknowledging that fallibility suggests the conclusion that any attempt to justify a claim to knowledge must lead to an infinite regress, to circularity, or remain a mere assumption begging the question. Klein (2007) defended the regress, and I have defended the loop (Lehrer, 2007) as maximizing explanation. Some have argued that fallible reliability is sufficient for knowledge. Reliability is possible without being infallible (Goldman, 1979). My objection to this way of dealing with the problem is that it fails to treat the role of defensible reasoning in knowledge. One may of course say that deduction of a conclusion from a false premise or belief is not a reliable way of arriving at truth, but the problem remains to explain when reasoning is sufficient for the defense of a knowledge claim and when it is not.

The answer that the reasoning must be reliable is insufficient. Given our fallibility and the compatibility of fallibility with reliability, it is clear that we might arrive at a false conclusion, and a false belief, by a reliable method. Our methods and processes are fallible and allow for error.

There have been attempts to avoid the Gettier problem by denying that justification is a condition for knowledge. Part of this has been based on appeal to the semantics of ordinary language of the words "know" and "justify." But my concern is not with semantics. It is with the role of knowledge in social practices and institutions, most notably, science, law, and philosophy. Here is where the justification game becomes salient, whatever words one may use to describe matters. The justification game of science, and other institutions guided by critical discourse, requires that the targets of knowledge be defensible. My concern is, and always has been, a concern with targets of knowledge whose acceptance satisfies the demands of critical reason, demands that include the capacity to defend accepting those targets of knowledge. However, the capacity to defend accepting those targets depends on internal states of the person in his evaluation system at the time the person knows.

PRIMITIVE KNOWLEDGE VERSUS DEFENSIBLE KNOWLEDGE

I do not deny that there may be more primitive forms of cognition where the target is not defensible. We may speak of infants, animals, and even insects as knowing things. I distinguished earlier (Lehrer, 2000a) between primitive and discursive knowledge. Sosa (2009) distinguished between animal and reflective knowledge with a similar motive. We may even say of the bee that it knows from responding to signals where to find a source of honey, but the bee, like the animal and infant, is ignorant of the practices of discerning truth from error by the use of reason. There is a form of knowledge that arises with the use of reason, however, in which we must use our powers of reason to defend what we accept as the targets of knowledge. We may be right, even regularly right in what we customarily believe, though unable to defend what we accept with the use of reason. In those cases, we lack an important kind of knowledge. We might call it scientific or rational knowledge. I choose to highlight the use of reason to *defend* accepting the content of knowledge in the justification game and call it *defensible knowledge*. Notice, finally, and crucially, that once this form of knowledge is before us, issues about whether to call the defensibility feature also *justification* is obviously a verbal dispute of no importance in epistemology whatever the interest in linguistic issues.

However, the confrontation with truth, our fallibility, and, therefore, the Gettier problem would remain for an account of defensible knowledge. Personal justification or defensibility, even given the reasonableness of the subject and the background system in meeting objections, would fail to provide a complete account of knowledge. Fallibility can result in failure, that is, error, even when we are reasonable. When we accept something, we place our trust in it, and when we claim to know it, we give others our authority for placing their trust in it as Austin (1962) remarked. But we can, even being trustworthy in accepting what we do, fail to obtain truth. Not all acceptances in a background evaluation system of a subject will be true. Consequently, not everything we are personally justified in accepting on the basis of what we accept will be true. Moreover, our reasonings in our evaluation system, the moves that we are ready to make in the justification game of defending something, will not always be sound reasonings. As the Gettier problem illustrated, some of those reasonings based on premises we accept will be based on false premises, even personally justified false premises. Finally, the preferences concerning what we accept to obtain truth may sometimes, contrary to our aims, involve a preference for accepting something false, that we are not deceived, over something true, that we are deceived, when deception succeeds against our best efforts to discover it. But defense of a target content based on error, though it may yield personal justification and personal defensibility as well, still fails to meet the demands of truth in a defense in the justification game of knowledge. Something more than personal justification for accepting something, and, as Gettier illustrated, even more than personal justification for accepting something that is true, must be added to obtain knowledge.

The claim, which I have been defending over a period of years, is that the kind of justification that yields knowledge must not depend *essentially* on any error in the background system of the subject. Knowledge of a given claim is, nevertheless, compatible with a good deal of inessential error in the background system of the subject. Indeed, knowledge is compatible with inconsistency in what the person believes in his background system, contrary to what I suggested earlier in (Lehrer, 1974). Bertrand Russell at one time accepted a set theory that was inconsistent. That did not in any way prevent him from knowing that he was Bertrand Russell or many of the other claims that were independent of what he accepted concerning sets. This reflection led to the constructive efforts I made to provide a theory of justification that explains when a justification a person has does not depend essentially on any error. I put this in another form as a constructive effort to explicate when and under what conditions the justification the person has for believing something is not defeated or refuted by any error in the background system of the person. My earliest effort to analyze knowledge as undefeated justified belief was an article co-authored with Paxson (Lehrer and Paxson, 1969), followed by a fuller treatment (Lehrer, 1974). John Pollock and I began discussion of the notion of defeasible reasoning. This occurred when we were very young and met in Rochester, New York in the early 1960s. He published a book on knowledge examining the issue (1974) in the same year that I published my own book on knowledge (Lehrer, 1974). I have no idea whether the idea was originally his or mine; it was probably his. Once you agree that reasoning must be admitted to be fallible, you must admit further that it is subject to error and the correction thereof. So the solution to the problem of knowledge was transformed by the problem Gettier raised into a problem of defeasible justification.

UNDEFEATED OR IRREFUTABLE JUSTIFICATION IN THE ULTRASYSTEM

What must be added to obtain defensible knowledge is a prophylactic against the ways in which the evaluation system may contain error that defeats personal justification. The proposal for an additional condition is one that takes us from the personal to the interpersonal, from the subjective to the intersubjective, from positive evaluation to correct evaluation. In short, we need to add a truth constraint. The truth constraint must be imposed on the content of the evaluation system. My proposal, recently presented in the *Theory of Knowledge*, 2nd edition (Lehrer, 2000b), is that we must consider a system based on the evaluation system of a person purified of errors in acceptances, reasonings, and preferences. To give it a name, I called it the *ultrasystem* of the person S. The *ultrasystem* of a person is the subsystem of the person containing only acceptances of what are true, sound reasonings from what are true, and preferences for what are true. Justification or defense of a target content, meeting all objections to it by beating or dismissing them on the basis of the *ultrasystem* of S, is a special form of justification, which I have called *undefeated* justification, but I now prefer to call *irrefutable justification*, or better even, *irrefutable defensibility*. It is important, however, to note that the *ultrasystem*, like the evaluation system of S of which it is a subsystem, is *not* a set of sentences but a set of actual states of S that are ready to meet objections to a target. The conclusion of our theory articulation is that knowledge is irrefutable defensibility of the target on the basis of the *ultrasystem* of S. I note that this account of irrefutability is strictly relativized to the system of S and amounts to the condition that there is no error in the system of S on which the justification of the target essentially depends. Dependence is revealed when elimination of false acceptance in the *ultrasystem* would refute all justifications of S for the target. Though the notion of irrefutability is relativized to the evaluation system of the subject, a person must accept or prefer to accept that he can meet external objections of others to the target. If this acceptance or preference for it is an error, then the person lacks irrefutable justification or defensibility in his *ultrasystem*. To

provide some continuity with past usage, I shall speak sometimes of *irrefutable justification* and at other times of *undefeated justification* because the two expressions describe the
same theory. An error that refutes a justification is the same
thing as an error that defeats a justification. My usage will depend on the emphasis I want to place on continuity with past
usage or with the novelty of the present one.

KNOWING THAT ONE KNOWS

This account, whatever the words used to describe it, leaves
us with two problems that are related and both pertain to
truth. The first arises from the fact that, being trustworthy
in what he accepts, though fallible, the person cannot know
what errors he is making in what he currently accepts. What
he accepts he considers to be true. If what he accepts is false,
he is just wrong. This has led to the objection that a person
is not in a position to know what remains in his *ultrasystem*
once errors have been eliminated from his evaluation
system. So the person is ignorant of the global contents of his
ultrasystem. It may be concluded that a person who knows
something on my account does not know that he knows because he does not know what remains in his *ultrasystem*.
This reasoning is faulty and the conclusion is false. It must
be granted that if a person knows something, this does not
entail that the person knows that he knows on my account.
But he may, nevertheless, know that he knows.

To know that he knows, he must accept that he knows
and be personally justified in accepting that he knows. So,
his evaluation system must give him the capacity to defend
the content that he knows against objections. Moreover, this

justification and defense must be sustained in his *ultrasystem* to yield irrefutable justification and defense of the content that he knows. Then he knows that he knows. But the subject does not have to know what the global contents of his *ultrasystem* are, capable of listing them, in order to know that his *ultrasystem* is adequate to meet objections to his target content to know. If it is adequate and he is personally justified in accepting that he knows, then he knows that he knows. In short, you do not have to know everything about a system to know that it is adequate to meet your purposes. I can know something about a system without knowing what all the contents of the system are.

EXEMPLAR REPRESENTATION AND THE TRUTH CONNECTION

So the account does not preclude knowing that one knows. There is, however, another objection to the theory concerning truth, and, indeed, concerning evidence of truth. Someone might object that theory is too hypothetical, too *iffy*, because it presupposes a connection of an *ultrasystem* with an evaluation system, a connection between acceptance that aims at truth and the attainment of truth. That a person is trustworthy in accepting what he does in accord with the norms of reason to obtain truth and avoid error is not sufficient, for it does not entail success in obtaining truth. Is there any connection whatever between how we represent the world in what we accept and the truth of what we accept? A secure truth connection between representation and the world represented results from the functional role of our experience in representation. In a number of chapters, I discuss exemplar representation of experience, which was the central notion in my most recent book, *Art, Self and Knowledge* (2011). Some appearance or sensation, for example, may be used as a symbol to present a class of appearances or sensations. The experience is used, as Hume (1888) suggested, to stand for a class of experiences, exhibiting, as a sample does, what the members of the class are like. Of course, the experience used as a sample or paradigm instance exhibiting what it represents is also a member of the class. So the experience functioning to exhibit what the things it represents are like reflexively represents itself, as I explain in other chapters.

I call the experience used in this way an *exemplar* and the process of using it as an exhibit of the experiences it represents *exemplarization*. The experience of red, for example, may be used as a term to represent a class of experiences. This is exemplar representation of a class. The exemplar is of course a member of the reference class. The exemplar used to stand for a class of entities functions like a term of reference that refers to the members of the exemplarized class. If it refers to members of the class, including itself, then it is true of members of the class, including itself. Exemplar representation yields a truth connection between experience and representation. Even Sellars, a materialist famous for his rejection of the *myth of the given* discussed in Chapter 5, seems to have advocated as I argue with Stern (Lehrer and Stern, 2000) and more recently (Lehrer, 2012b) that an experience may come to exhibit what the represented state is like so that the subject can report the existence of the state from the experience of it. Some find it odd to think of an exemplar, which may be a physical state, functioning like a sample to refer or be true of what it stands for. This is the result of thinking of the exemplar as lacking syntax. It may, however, function in the language of thought as a predicate does in language. The sensation may stand in functionally for the referential and inferential roles of a predicate, as I shall explain in Chapter 4.

When an experience of a sensation occurs, it may, with the proper attention to what it is like, become an exemplar representation of a class of sensations by itself without the intermediary of words. Indeed, there may be no word in language that represents what the exemplarized sensation represents. I concede, however, that the conversion of exemplar representation into a predicate, even a predicate solely in thought, may be achieved, as Hume again noted, by the association of an exemplar representation with a word. The importance of such an association should not lead one to think that the exemplar depends on an association with a word to become a term of representation of a class of entities. On the contrary, a person may generalize from an exemplar, using it as an exemplar exhibit of a class or entities it stands for, even if the person cannot find a word that refers to that class. Once the formal role of the exemplar, a predicative role, is added to the functional role of exhibiting what entities the exemplar stands for, it becomes easier to accept the claim that the exemplar predicate refers to and is true of the entities of which it is predicated, including, reflexively, itself.

Let us call the kind of exemplarization of an experience to stand for a class of experiences, which allows for application of the exemplar to those experiences as a predicate *ostensive predication*. It supplies a truth connection and shows us what a truth connection is like in a way that no verbal description of the truth connection can achieve. It shows us something beyond any description of the connection because the truth of the exemplar predicate results from the role of the exemplar to show us something beyond discourse as I explain in Chapter 4. However, the truth connection of experiences onto experiences leaves us with the need to explain the truth connection of experiences with entities beyond themselves. I argue that the exemplar experience, which reflexively refers to itself as well as other experiences by exhibiting what they are like, radiates outward to refer to external entities in the world functioning to exhibit what they are like for us in Chapter 2.

Part of how we conceive of objects in the empirical world is in terms of the look, smell, and feel of them, in short, in terms of experiences that may be exemplarized to reveal what objects of the external world are like at the same time that they reveal what the experiences themselves are like. When the experiences are exemplarized to represent things other than experiences, the security of reflexive representation is sacrificed. A risk of error is introduced. Notice that the application of the exemplar, as a representation of other experiences, also takes us beyond reflexive representation to intentionality of reference and carries a risk of error. When our experience becomes representational, when it functions to exhibit what something beyond itself is like, we confront our fallibility. There is more to what the thing represented is like than can be exhibited by the exemplar. This implies that representation of the existence of something by an exemplar is defeasible. Though the exemplar representation has a functional role in the meaning of discourse about the external object, exhibiting what it is like, the representation is neither a logically necessary nor a sufficient condition of the meaning. The connection with meaning resulting from the functional role has a semantically stochastic or probability role that is constitutive. The conditional probability that the described object will manifest a member of the exemplar represented class of experiences is part of the meaning of the word used to describe the object.

EXEMPLARS AS EVIDENCE

Does use of the exemplar to represent things beyond itself sacrifice the capacity of the representation to provide us with evidence for accepting the truth of the existence of those external objects? Have we lost the evidence of truth? The evidence of truth is sustained, even if less secure, by the extension, the radiation, of exemplar representation to exhibit how we conceive of the external objects. The exemplar representation becomes part of what we mean when we claim that the objects exist. This claim depends on a functional theory of meaning according to how we apply our words to the external world. The functional role of the exemplar makes it a constituent of meaning. Meaning gives us truth conditions. The exemplar representation is evidence of truth because it is a component of meaning. We apply words to the external world in terms of how we experience the world, how the objects of the world appear, smell, and feel. So our claims based on the evidence of those experiences are evidence of the truth of what we mean by our words and thoughts about the world.

What is the role of exemplar representation in defensible knowledge and the justification game? Defensible knowledge is irrefutable justification or irrefutable defensibility of the target content of knowledge. Personal justification or defensibility requires the capacity of the evaluation system of the person to meet objections by beating them or dismissing them. One central objection to many target contents, especially perceptual contents, is that the replies to objections provided by the evaluation system of the person are disconnected from truth about the external world. The argument above is the answer to the disconnection or isolation objection that arises both locally in providing replies to objections to a target content and more generally as an objection to a theory of defensible knowledge based on a background system of what a person accepts, prefers to accept, and reasons therefrom. We have added a constraint on personal justification to convert it to knowledge that it be irrefutable, sustained in an *ultrasystem* cleansed of error. To know that one knows depends on knowing that is sustained in the *ultrasystem* cleansed of error with only truth remaining. At this level, justification depends on knowing that what one accepts to meet objections is truth connected. Exemplar predication supplies evidence of the truth connection. It supplies the experiential *premises* that are empirical evidence of truth. Defensible knowledge must answer the objection that the background system of the subject is isolated from reality and truth. The answer is exemplar representation. My goal in this book is to elaborate this answer to account for our knowledge of the world.

2

PERCEPTUAL KNOWLEDGE

OF THE EXTERNAL WORLD

COHERENCE AND CONNECTION
WITH EXPERIENCE

This chapter concerns the justification and defense of perceptual knowledge claims. One objection to coherence theories of justification is that coherence with a background system does not provide a connection with experience that explains how we know. This objection, the disconnection or isolation objection, is met in this chapter. The theory of defensible knowledge as undefeated or irrefutable justification developed in this book requires answering the disconnection objection as a condition of justification. The isolation objection was raised by Moser (1989) in his insightful discussion of coherence theories of justification. It was further discussed by Conee (1994).

The reply to the objection is that conscious experience provides a representation of experience that becomes part of the meaning and, therefore, evidence for the truth of the perceptual claim. Connection with experience in the background system, the evaluation system, is the result of attending to experience in such a way that the experience itself becomes a vehicle of representation accepted into the background system to meet the disconnection or isolation objection. In what follows, I focus as Reid (1863) did on the sensation of smell as the conscious experience that provides a premise of evidence. My reason for selecting smelling is that it is often eclipsed in epistemological discussion by vision and touch and, most critically, because a strong smell, like that of a skunk discussed below, directs attention to itself in a way that converts the sensation into a representation of what it is like. I do not claim that all conscious experience contains a representation of what it is like. Sometimes conscious experience, both visual and tactual, passes through the mind without calling attention to what it is like. Indeed, as Stubenberg (1998) argued, what it means to *have* such qualities of experience is problematic. Though the experience may evoke some response, it does not become a representation of what it is like in itself. Without such representation, the experience is not available as a premise in defense of a target perceptual claim. You need a representation to defend a conclusion. However, as I shall explain below, the capacity for such representation may play a role in defensibility and justification. Though I have spoken of undefeated justification and irrefutable justification as the same, I use the notion of undefeated justification in this chapter to indicate how the representation of experience can become part of a background system in my earlier formulation of knowledge as undefeated justification.

Conscious experience of the sensation of smell provides exemplars of the sensation exhibiting to us what they are like. These exemplars of experiences can become vehicles or terms of representation and meaning. I call this *exemplar representation* and the process *exemplarization* (Lehrer, 2011). The notion of exemplarization is indebted to Hume (1888) and Goodman (1968). I modify the notion here to apply to the sensation of smell. Exemplar representation differs from verbal representation because the exemplar, like a sample, exhibits what the represented items smell like—a perfume, a spice, or an animal. The exemplar represents the sensation and, at the same, represents an external object: my example is the spray of a skunk exhibiting what a skunk smells like. The exemplar is part of the meaning and conception of the external object. This solves the problem, as Reid insisted, of how experience of smell justifies perceptual belief in the existence of external objects (1863, pp. 105–108). The meaning of thought and discourse about external objects is not exhausted by the exemplarization of the sensation of smell, but the exemplar becomes evidence of their existence as part of the meaning of what they smell like. The evidence and justification of the exemplar is fallible and defeasible. However, exemplar justification, when undefeated by error in the way it coheres with a background system, becomes knowledge of the external world.

AN EXAMPLE: THE SMELL OF A SKUNK

The object of this chapter is to explain the relationship between perception, sensory representation, and knowledge. I shall begin with the example of a perception of smell. My reason for beginning with smell is that the role of sensation may force attention and be impossible to ignore in the perception of objects perceived by smell. Here is the example: Imagine that Dante is walking in the woods when a skunk, nearby but out of sight, suddenly sprays his distinctive odor. Here are facts about Dante:

1. Dante does not see the skunk but experiences the unpleasant sensation.
2. Dante does not know what a skunk smells like or even that such an animal exists.
3. Dante does not know that the smell is the smell of a skunk or that he smells a skunk.
4. Dante knows what the sensation in itself is like.
5. Dante knows that the sensation is of an external odor from something outside.
6. Dante does not know that the sensation of an external odor from something outside is the smell of the spray of a skunk.
7. Nevertheless, Dante smells the spray of a skunk when he experiences the sensation.

The point is that Dante can have a sensation of smell, of an odor he cannot ignore, and know what the sensation of smell is like without knowing what causes the sensation of smell.

Now let us add a second chapter to our example.

8. Dante is with an experienced hiker, Beatrice, who tells him that what he smells is the spray of a skunk.
7. Dante then identifies the sensation of the odor as the smell of a spray of a skunk.
9. Dante knows that there is a skunk within spraying distance.

So Dante initially experiences an offensive sensation of smell. He knows what the offensive sensation of smell is like in itself. He also knows that the sensation is an external odor. He does not initially know that the odor is the smell of a skunk, but he knows that there is an external odor and what that odor is like from his sensory experience, his olfactory sensation, before he knows that the smell is the smell of skunk.

Dante experiences an offensive, indeed noxious, sensation in his nose. He smells an odor outside himself from the sensation in his nose. He perceives an odor outside himself from the sensation in his nose. Dante initially knows that he smells something and what the smell is like, at least what the sensation of the smell is like, before he knows anything more about the smell. When Beatrice tells him it is the smell of the spray of a skunk, he perceives that it is the smell of the spray of a skunk as a result, and if she is trustworthy, he knows from her testimony that it is the smell of the spray of a skunk and that a skunk is within smelling distance. He may be ignorant of what a skunk is like other than how the spray of a skunk smells.

KNOWING WHAT A SENSATION OF SMELL IS LIKE

However, before Dante knows anything about the skunk, he knows something about what the smell is like, what the sensation of it is like. This raises the question of what minimal knowledge a person must have of what an object is like to smell or perceive the object. To put the matter in a more classical first person form, to be perceptually acquainted with an object, I must know something about what it is like. Perhaps that is what has led philosophers, notably Russell (1910–1911), to speak about knowledge by acquaintance. If acquaintance is a form of knowledge, then acquaintance must show us what the object of acquaintance is like. If acquaintance with an object shows us what the object is like and provides us with some knowledge of what it is like, then we must have some conception of what it is like. To be shown what something is like and thereby to come to know what it is like, we must have the capacity to conceive of what it is like. So acquaintance must somehow carry some minimal form of conception along with it.

Sellars taught us in his discussion of the myth of the given that having a sense experience does not entail having a conception of what it is like (1963a). So the experience of acquaintance must supply a vehicle for conceiving of what it is like to yield knowledge. Now one might imagine that we are innately supplied with conceptions of every character of sensory experience. That is not very plausible, however. It implies, for example, that we are innately supplied with conceptions of what all works of art, past, present, and future, are like without having perceived them, indeed, without having perceived any work of art. That is very implausible. There is something about what a work of art is like that you do not know until you have experienced it. A similar point can be made about other sensory experiences. Moreover, being acquainted with something, as Russell's terminology of knowledge by acquaintance suggests, results in some knowledge of what it is like.

REPRESENTING EXPERIENCE:
HISTORICAL REFLECTIONS

To be acquainted with something somehow supplies us with the means of knowing what it is like. My proposal is that the experience becomes the vehicle for representing or conceiving of what it is like. In this way, the experience becomes a term of representation that is true of itself. The fundamental idea behind this proposal comes from Hume (1888). He was puzzled by the possibility of general ideas and how we come to have them from individual impressions. His solution was that the individual impression is used to stand for a class of impressions. The individual impression thus becomes a general idea as it stands for a general class of impressions. It is then associated with some general word that applies to those impressions. We might say that this generalized impression becomes part of the meaning of the general word. The meaning of the word "red" as applied to impressions, according to Hume, consists of an individual impression generalized to stand for the class of objects we call "red." The meaning, rather than being achieved by definition, is achieved by generalizing.

In an attempt to defend logical positivism, Schlick later proposed that an individual experience could be the meaning of a word (1979). He argued that a word could be true of an experience by virtue of the meaning of the word because the experience was the meaning of the word. He was more concerned with the individual demonstrative character of such words than any general character. So, "red here now," was his example. It is clear, however, that the use of the word "red" appears to involve a general word referring to a class of members. I do not mention this as a critical account, but instead as acknowledging a contribution to the idea that an individual experience can constitute the meaning of a word or expression. Moreover, the question whether an individual experience can constitute the meaning of a word without becoming a general idea or conception is an important one. We shall return to a discussion of that issue below.

Goodman (1968) introduced the most explicit development of Hume's idea. Goodman introduced the notion of *exemplification* to characterize the special symbolic and cognitive role an individual, a sample, can acquire. Here is Goodman's account of exemplification: Consider a color sample of paint. Suppose that you asked me to show you the color International Klein Blue, the color of a famous painting by Yves Klein. I show you a sample. You take the sample to refer to a color property that the sample exemplifies. The sample is used to pick out the property it exemplifies. What is special about Goodman's account is the symbolic role of the sample in exemplification. The sample used to refer to the property becomes a symbol. This is so without a word being used to refer to the property. So the sample itself is a symbol because it is referential. I think this is an important insight in Goodman. An item of experience of an individual work of art can be used referentially to pick out a character of that object in a context, for example a property that the item possesses. The individual item of experience becomes a symbol referring to a property according to Goodman and indirectly to other individuals that possess that property.

What is common to the proposals of Hume and Goodman is the idea that an individual experience can become a symbol by being used to refer to a property or a class of individuals. I have suggested that the nominalism of Hume and Goodman would be better served by dropping the reference to properties, and even predicates. The notion of a property is not used in Hume's account and is only used paraphrastically in Goodman's to refer to predicates. Goodman's account allows an individual item of experience to refer to something beyond experiences. This will prove important for understanding the symbolic role of the individual experience in perception. I now turn to my (Lehrer, 2011) account of that symbolic role.

EXEMPLAR REPRESENTATION AND EXEMPLARIZATION

I call the individual item that plays the symbolic role of representing a class of individuals an *exemplar*. I call the process of using the exemplar to represent a class of objects *exemplarization*. The process of exemplarization is one of using an exemplar to stand for objects it represents and to which it refers. The special feature of exemplarization in representations is that it exhibits what the objects belonging to the class are like. In that way, it differs from a word or some conventional symbol that is usually unlike the things it represents. However, the exemplar functions like a word in referring to objects it stands for or represents. Moreover, just as a word, like "blue," is true of the objects it represents, so the exemplar is true of the objects it represents. What makes exemplarization special is the way in which the exemplar is used to achieve representation. It represents the objects, showing us what they are like, being what they are like itself.

It is useful to contrast my notion of exemplarization with Goodman's notion of exemplification. The contrast is subtle. For Goodman, the exemplar, or the sample, refers indirectly to individuals by referring to a property the individuals exemplify. So his account of exemplification presupposes the notion of a property as well as the notion of an individual exemplifying a property. It is odd that Goodman, who was so strongly committed to nominalism, should have presupposed these notions. I have argued that these presuppositions, even if they can be paraphrased in a way compatible with nominalism, are unnecessary in an account of how the exemplar represents what it does.

The process of exemplarization presupposes some psychological capacities and activities. First of all, attention must be focused on the exemplar. The unnoticed exemplar cannot be the basis of exemplarization. Secondly, converting the exemplar into a general symbol requires generalizing from the exemplar to a class of objects. Thirdly, the objects represented must be distinguished from the objects not represented. So exemplarization involves the psychological processes of attending to the exemplar, generalizing from the exemplar, and distinguishing the exemplar from those objects not referred to by it. This account of exemplarization, or exemplar reference, assumes that it is intelligible to suppose that someone generalizes from an individual to others without referring to some property as the basis of generalization.

I assume that the activity of generalizing is more basic than the notion or activity of recognizing a property. In short, the description of exemplarization is compatible with nominalism and a psychology based upon it. Exemplar representation, unlike Goodman's notion of exemplification, has the fundamental feature that the exemplar itself is used as a symbol instantiated by the objects to which it refers. Of special interest is the fact that the exemplar refers to and represents itself as well as other objects. It is, therefore, true of itself. On Goodman's account, the property referred to by an exemplar might be true of the items exemplified by the property or instantiated by some predicate designating the property. But the exemplar or sample is not itself true of the items exemplified on Goodman's account. It is the property or predicate referred to by the sample, not the sample itself, that is true of the sample. A feature of the theory of exemplarization is that the exemplar becomes a genuine symbol that is instantiated and is true of objects to which it refers. I shall at the end turn to the relation between exemplar representation and linguistic representation. Here I only note in passing, following Reid (1863, p. 364), and later Putnam (1975), that a person often uses a vehicle of linguistic representation to refer to what another uses it to refer to, delegating the role of reference to the other without further knowledge of what object the other has referred to. In this way, reference initiated by an individual from exemplar representation may play a role in the social practice of the reference of language, as I shall explain below.

PERCEPTUAL KNOWLEDGE AND EXEMPLARS

I now want to argue that the notion of exemplar representation is central to an explanation of how we know what we perceive. Indeed, I shall propose that this notion of exemplar representation provides a solution to the traditional problem of our knowledge of the external world. In order to take the problem seriously, I shall make a concession to those philosophers influenced by Hume, later phenomenalists, and the earlier logical positivists, who assumed that the starting point of our knowledge of the external world must be representations of our conscious awareness of the character of sensory experience. I adopt this starting point to show that this assumption does not lead to skepticism. I assume that this will be considered an advantage of the theory I present in replying to an opponent. It is important to concede as many premises to the opponent as possible to avoid begging the question.

So let us suppose that we must begin our quest of knowledge of the external world with representations of sensory states, sensations of smell, for example. Now let us suppose, following the phenomenalist tradition, that the first premises of knowledge consist of representations concerning the phenomenal character of our experience. It is important to recognize that this is not a claim about the psychological origin of perception but about the justification of perceptual claims. Indeed, there is no inconsistency in conceding that some psychological mechanism supplies us with some initial representations of the external world while denying that such representations are justified. Assumptions about the etiology of such a representation do not prove that the representation is justified by its origin. To accommodate the phenomenalists, I begin with their assumption that justification takes as initial premises representations and beliefs about the character of sensory experience.

Suppose that we begin the task of justification with sensory experience and, more specifically, with the individual quality of sensory experience. Sellars, as we noted, argued convincingly that the mere awareness of sensory experience does not entail that we have a conception of what it is like. Put in phenomenalist terms, there is a distinction between sensing a sense datum or a sense impression and having a conception or representation of what it is like. In the preceding remarks about exemplar representation, we find a quick solution to the problem of the representation of a sensory experience. Once attention is directed to the sensory experience, it may become the exemplar of exemplar representation. Our sensations become instances of exemplar representation. The sensation used as an exemplar to refer to sensations has the additional feature of also referring to itself. In this case, the reference of the exemplar to itself is reflexive, as others such as Ismael (2007) and Fürst (2014), and later Tolliver and myself (Lehrer and Tolliver, 2014), have noted. The reflexive referential character of the exemplar to itself must be distinguished from disquotation, which is a relation between an item in quotation marks and another item that is not in quotation marks. Disquotational theories, for example Papineau (2002), are similar to reflexive theory, but they are not the same in their consequences concerning truth and reference. According to reflexive theory, the exemplar refers to itself, and being a term of reference that is true of the things to which it refers, it is also true of itself. Perhaps this is one reason why Hume and his followers may have thought that all representations of our sense data or sense impressions were more evident or certain, more secure from error, than all representations of the external world. Exemplar representation creates a reflexive truth connection.

The reflexive character of exemplar representation along with its truth-ensuring feature may explain why we use the word "know" in describing our response to a sensory experience. When a person experiences a sensation, we say that the person knows what it is like. Perhaps this is due to the reflexive character of exemplar representation. It is important to notice that having the experience does not logically entail exemplar representation. Exemplar representation involves a cognitive process of using an exemplar referentially, and that process supplements the experience. Though this is controversial, consider the initial moments of awakening when you are barely conscious and cognitive processing does not yet enable you to represent or to know what the conscious experience is like. You smell an odor, for example, but cannot identify it. In this case, you smell something though you do not yet have any conception or representation of the sensation of the odor. Some unfortunate individuals with brain lesions that block all cognitive functioning may never get beyond that form of consciousness. They have sensations without any conception of them.

Exemplarization of sensations, of sense data, and of sense impressions supplies exemplar representations of them. The reflexive character of the representation enables us to know what they are like. There is a question about the justification of these representations, and it is not beyond controversy. But one might assume that the reflexive character of the representations supplies a security of truth as the exemplar warrants accepting such representations of experience as the initial premises of all justification about the world. I make no major claims for this argument except to note that the reflexive character of exemplar representation avoids one kind of error. When one compares one thing to another, whether to other individuals, predicates, or properties, one confronts the possibility of error in making the comparison. Reflexivity avoids that source of error.

JUSTIFICATION AND DEFENSE

Now we confront the problem of proceeding to justify and defend claims about the external world on the basis of these exemplarized representations of sensory experience. One attempt to do so, which was the motivation for the phenomenalists, was to reduce the premises about the external world to premises about sensory experience. The program proved to be a failure. However, once we recognize that exemplar representation is the basis of the justification of the initial premises about sensory experience, we have supplied ourselves with the means for justification that goes beyond those premises. The reason is that exemplar representation involves the notion of using one thing to refer to another. Without the notion of reference, we lack a representation of the sensory experience itself. Though I have placed great emphasis on the reflexive character of exemplar representation, the notion of reference is presupposed. It is natural, starting with Hume, to assume that sense impressions or sensory data are used to refer to or stand for other sensory impressions or sensory data. But where is the argument that the exemplars of experience cannot be used to refer to anything beyond experiences? There is no such argument. Thus, once it is established that exemplar representation requires that a person have the capacity to use an exemplar to refer to something beyond itself, then it must be admitted that they can be used to refer to the external world.

Truth security is compromised once an exemplar of sensation is used to refer to something beyond itself, extending beyond reflexivity, even when an exemplar of experience is only used to refer to other experiences a subject is not currently undergoing. In short, exemplar representation carries with it intentionality, that is, reference to things beyond what is presently experienced. Once this is noticed, the door of exemplar representation opens to the external world.

Consider our example of the sensation of the odor of skunk. As an exemplar used for the purposes of exemplar representation, the exemplar is used to refer by exhibiting what the things it refers to are like. One might ask what things the exemplar sensation refers to. If we restrict ourselves to the phenomenalist form of representation, the exemplar will be used to represent a class of sensations that are like the exemplar. That form of representation is reflexive when the exemplar is used to refer to itself. But exemplar representation transcends reflexivity. It also refers to other sensations of odor of the skunk represented by the exemplar. Having asked what things the exemplar is used to represent, it becomes obvious that the phenomenalist restriction, which mandates that exemplars only represent sensory items, is groundless.

An exemplar may be used to represent and refer to many different kinds of things. The sensation of the odor of a skunk, our example, may be used to represent the spray of a skunk, and, indirectly, a skunk. You think of the sensation and think that is what the spray of a skunk is like. Words and other vehicles of representation, including the exemplars of experience, may be used in different ways to refer to different kinds of objects. A sensory experience may show us what an external odor is like. The sensation of the odor of the spray of a skunk can show us what the spray is like. Proceeding beyond sensations of smell to other appearances, we recognize that appearances, though complex, show us what external objects are like. A mistake of the phenomenalist was to assume that a sense datum could only show us what other sense data are like. In fact, sense data or sensations show us what external objects are like—the spray of a skunk, for example. As they function to show us what the external objects are like for us, we may use them as exemplar exhibits for the exemplar representation of the external objects.

VARIETIES OF EXEMPLAR REPRESENTATION

Distinctions are in order concerning the objects represented by the exemplar of experience. The sensation may be exemplarized to represent sensations functioning as an exhibit that stands for sensations. The exemplar represents sensations in this form of representation by showing what the represented sensations are like. Call this form of representation of sensation *ostensive* exemplarization. The exemplar sensation is used as a term or vehicle of representation referring to sensations as instances. The exemplar itself is an instance. The exemplar represents itself as well as other sensations. There is in this case a loop of reflexive self-representation and self-reference. The application of the exemplar to itself yields a conditional or contingent guarantee of truth or incorrigibility. If a sensation is exemplarized and used as an exhibit to represent a plurality of sensations, then it represents (stands for, refers to) and is true of itself. That is conditionally guaranteed. The guarantee of truth depends on the direct use of the exemplar sensation to represent sensations including itself without the intervention and mediation of language predicates. As we noted, Goodman introduced the notion of using an experience as a symbol in his notion of exemplification. But, as the term exemplification suggests, the experience becomes a symbol by referring to some property or language predicate the experience exemplifies or instantiates. Taking the predicate as illustration, the instantiation of the predicate mediates the symbolic use of the experience. This mediation introduces the hazards of language predicate instantiation into the guarantee of truth. The mediation of predicates to represent truth about sensory experience eliminates the reflexive truth security of exemplar representation. The mediation of language, as phenomenalists and positivists eventually conceded, undermines the quest for incorrigibility in the initial descriptions of sensory experience.

Having considered the exemplars of sensation to represent sensations, we turn to radiation of exemplarization of the exemplars to represent external objects. The exemplar sensation may be exemplarized to represent something external to the sensation, initially, a quality in the external world. Consider the odor of the spray of the skunk in the external world that Dante smells when he is ignorant of the source of the odor. He smells the odor when he does not know anything about skunks. There is a stink, a disagreeable odor, experienced in his sensation of smell. He does not know where the odor is from or what object is producing it, but he smells the odor out there. Dante represents the odor in terms of the sensation. His conception and knowledge of the odor may be limited to the sensation that exhibits what the odor is like, and his conception, however vague, of the odor being out there in the environment. The sensation is exemplarized to represent the external quality. I shall call this *quality exemplarization*.

The distinction between sensation exemplarization and quality exemplarization is not intended to describe temporal stages of representation, that is, I do not assume that the formation of the first precedes the second. Moreover, the same sensation used as a term of representation of a sensation and a quality shows us that the exemplar, like other terms of representation, words most notably, can ambiguously represent different objects, sensations, or external qualities, and, as we shall next discuss, external objects that have those qualities. Nevertheless, the exemplar, as a term or vehicle of exemplar representation, is also part of our conception of sensation and quality. The sensation has a functional role in conception and representation of exhibiting what the sensation and quality is like. By playing this role it enables the subject to identify the sensations or qualities it represents.

Return again to our example of smelling the skunk. There is the exemplarization of the sensation converting it into a representation of sensations, a conception of what the sensations are like, functioning as an exhibit of what they are like. The same sensation may be used as an exemplar to represent a quality, an odor, becoming part of our conception of it, exhibiting what it is like. The exemplar of representation ambiguously represents both the sensation and the quality. The quality is something external, but knowing what the quality is like depends on knowing what the sensation is like, for the sensation shows us what the quality is like.

Moreover, since the quality is in fact a quality of the skunk, the sensation that represents the quality may also be part of how Dante conceives of or represents a skunk. I call this *object exemplarization*. A person like Dante informed by Beatrice about skunks, who now has a conception of skunks that goes beyond the quality experienced, still conceives of skunks in terms of the exemplarized sensation of the odor. There is more to a skunk than the way it smells, but the smell of a skunk, the odor, is nevertheless part of Dante's conception of a skunk. If we have experienced the smell of skunk like Dante, we also conceive of a skunk in terms of how it smells and the obnoxious sensation. It is interesting that the German language builds this into the word used to name a skunk. The word is *stinktier*.

EXEMPLARS AND KNOWLEDGE OF THE EXTERNAL WORLD

We are now left with the task of explaining how smelling can give us knowledge of the external world, that is, of explaining how the exemplarized sensory experiences can provide us with knowledge of what the external objects are like. Truth is a condition of knowledge, and so we must explain how sensory representation in terms of the exemplar is connected with truth. When we use the exemplars of sensory experience to represent or refer to the sensory experience itself, there is a truth security obtained from the reflexivity that entitles us to speak of knowing what the experience is like. But representation or reference beyond that sacrifices the truth security of reflexivity. That leaves us with the question of what justification we have for claiming to know of the existence of the external object from the exemplar representation of it.

The answer to this question is simple. Exemplar representation of the object uses the exemplar as a symbol to refer to the external object by exhibiting what the external object is like. If we think of the meaning of the exemplar as the role that it plays in our representational system, the exemplar refers to the external object as part of its meaning in exemplar representation. Put another way, the exemplar is true of the objects to which it refers by virtue of the meaning of the exemplar. We have not yet turned to the issue of the relationship between word representation and exemplar representation, but we note here that the exemplar can be true of objects as a result of the referential meaning of the exemplar representation. Exemplar representation uses the exemplar to represent the things to which it refers in a special way. It exhibits something about what the represented objects are like. A sensation shows us what a skunk smells like when exemplarized to represent the odor of a skunk. The truth security is less than that of the sensation referring to itself. The truth connection between the exemplar of smell and the external object does not have the truth security of reflexive representation. The sensation used to represent the smell of an object is something distinct from the object it represents, which allows for the possibility of error. What is interesting about the case, however, is that the representational function or meaning of the exemplar representation of the odor of a skunk only succeeds because the sensation refers as an exemplar of the odor. Exemplar representation brings us a truth connection as a success condition of the representational meaning or function of the term.

Now let us turn to the question of the connection between exemplar representation and knowledge. The truth connection resulting from the exemplar representation in the case in which the representation is reflexive protects us from error. The success of the exemplar referring to itself, as a condition of using it as a term of representation, yields security from error. That may explain why it is natural to use the word "know" as we do when we remark that a person who has a sensation knows what it is like. To know what something is like requires that the subject have some conception or representation of what it is like, and exemplar representation of the experienced sensation ensures that the exhibit refers to itself as well as other members of the class. As a result of referring to itself, it is true of itself. Because this kind of exemplar representation yields a true conception of what the sensation is like, it is natural to call it knowing what the sensation is like.

However, this case of sensation exemplarization is special, and we now turn from reflexive representation to forms of exemplar representation in which the exemplar is used to represent things beyond itself. The exemplarization of the sensation of smell to represent the odor of a skunk may be usefully compared to other sense modalities in which the exemplarization of sensory experiences represents external objects. One similar example is a sensation of color used as an exemplar to represent a physical object such as the paint on a surface by exhibiting what it looks like. Another is the visual appearance of a skunk as an exemplar to represent a skunk by showing us what it looks like. Or, more theoretically, the appearance of an electron photograph to show us what a ribosome on the surface of a cell is like. The latter case, which I discuss in an earlier work (Lehrer, 2011), is interesting because a conceptual understanding, or even a hypothetical conjecture of what the surface of the cell is like, was absent prior to the special use of the electron microscope to produce digital information articulated in a photograph. In this case, it becomes apparent that the sensory appearance of the photograph is part and parcel of our conception of the surface and how we represent it. The critical point is that the experience of the sensation or appearance can function as part of the meaning of our conception of a skunk, a paint, or a ribosome as a result of exhibiting what these physical objects are like. At the same time, it is a parcel of information, a term of reference, representing the objects. This is the basis of a solution to the problem of how experience of sensations and appearances can be part of the meaning of our representations of external objects and theoretical entities. The solution is that the sensory experiences can function as exemplars representing entities and referring to them by exhibiting what an experience of them is like. The exemplarized experiences can become part of the meaning, as I shall explain below, of our representation of the entities exhibited.

Suppose we accept the extension of exemplar representation to external objects and theoretical entities. How does exemplar representation get converted to knowledge? The conversion requires my analysis of defensible knowledge articulated in the previous chapter. Those who would defend an externalist or reliabilist conception of knowledge might find that the only remaining question is whether the functional process of exemplarizing sensory experiences to represent external things is reliable. If it is a reliable form of representation, the step to knowledge for them is short and quick. However, from my standpoint, the reliabilist rush to knowledge trips over itself. It fails to meet Hume's simple objection that we will by proceeding in this way fail to justify acceptance of the necessary additional premise that such exemplar representation is reliably truth connected. We may say that *if* such representation is reliably truth connected, we have knowledge, at least of a simple and primitive form, but what evidence or reason do we have for thinking it is reliably truth connected? If we cannot answer the question, then our claim to knowledge is left hanging on a hypothetical *if*. Until we pass beyond this *if*, we must acknowledge a lack of transparency, a presence of opacity, in the claim to knowledge.

Moreover, the opacity is readily removed. Our evidence for the connection is contained in the character of exemplar representation, that is, in the way such representation functions. The exemplar functions to represent the things it does, whether subjective states or objective ones, by exhibiting what the things referred to are like as a condition of the meaning of the exemplar representation. This is not a proof that the things exist, but it is evidence for their existence. Dante may ask himself whether he smells a skunk when he experiences the stinking odor, and he could be deceived when the odor is hallucinatory. But Dante is not deceived in thinking his sensation is evidence of the existence of a skunk nearby. On the contrary, the experience that Dante is having of a sensation of smell is an experience of what it is like to smell a skunk. There remains the problem of the relation of subjective experience to external ontology. Dante is aware of the problem when he looks around for a skunk producing the spray. Dante, even if hallucinating the external odor from the sensation, has evidence he smells a skunk nearby. The sensation is an exemplar exhibiting what it is like to smell the odor of a skunk. It exhibits to Dante what the odor is like and refers to it. Evidence results from the functional role of the sensation in the conception of the quality of the external object exhibiting what the object is like. Deceived or not, the sensation is evidence for Dante of the existence of the external thing.

Exemplar representation supplies a person with evidence of the existence of external things as a result of the role of the exemplar in exhibiting what the external thing is like. This is not by itself sufficient against a skeptic. Our justification and evidence converts to knowledge, as I have explained in the preceding chapter and more fully elsewhere (Lehrer, 2000b), when we can meet objections in terms of our background system in a way that is not defeated by error. Exemplarization is not the last step in the quest for knowledge or proof that the skeptic is wrong. It is an effective step in the game of justification. Assuming that we are trustworthy in what we accept, which we have reason to think we are, we know that the skeptic is wrong and that we have knowledge, even though appealing to such knowledge would beg the question against the skeptic. Exemplar representation provides the experiential knot around the keystone acceptance of our trustworthiness tying experience and theory up, down, and together in a loop.

EXEMPLAR REPRESENTATION AND LINGUISTIC DESCRIPTION

I conclude with a reflection on the relation between exemplar representation and other forms of representation, most notably linguistic representation. The use of the exemplar as a vehicle of representation has the advantage of exhibiting what the represented object is like as a means of representation. An exemplar need not be something private. It may be a public object like a sample of paint. Passing from an exemplar to a word as a term of representation has the disadvantage that it deprives us, in most cases, of a representation that shows us what the represented object is like. However, the word has the advantage of supplying a representation with inferential connections. As we touch on linguistic representation, we encounter the question of the role of exemplar representation in linguistic representation. The issue has special importance when we later consider the interpersonal defense of representation in language involving the social discourse of objection and reply of the justification game.

What is the role of exemplar representation in linguistic representation? The fundamental role of the exemplar in linguistic representation is transferred from the role it plays in exemplar representation, namely, of showing or exhibiting what the represented object is like. As it exhibits what the represented object is like, it shows us how to pick out the referents of the term from our experience and becomes part of the meaning of the term. I have suggested with Wagner (Lehrer and Wagner, 1981) a mathematical theory of interpersonal meaning as the consensual aggregate found with a fixed-point vector of consensual weights of respect that members of a linguistic community give to each other. In development of the consensual theory of word meaning with Adrienne Lehrer, (Lehrer, A., and K. Lehrer, 1995, 1998, 2009), I argued that meaning should be viewed as vectors, following Ziff (1972), of application of a word, which we called *reference*, combined with vectors of semantic relations, which we called *sense*. Terminology aside, the idea is that how people apply a term, as well as how they understand the semantic relations between terms, should be understood as involving indeterminacy, understood stochastically, which allows for differences in how different individuals apply terms and relate terms semantically. The exemplar representation plays a role in how the term is applied and may, as a result, influence semantic connections in the idiolects of individuals. Moreover, there is commitment to a consensual aggregation of such vectors of application and inference in the consensual meaning of the communal language based on the weights individuals assign to others. The commitment results from the weights that an individual gives to others that generate the consensual aggregate to which individuals, as a consequence of their assigning weights, give authority. The delegation of authority of meaning was suggested by Reid and made noteworthy by Putnam as we noted above.

The consequence of a combination of individual exemplar representation with consensual representation is a theory that incorporates individual exemplarization with social delegation to external authority. Individual exemplarization in representation may be overridden in the social aggregate that incorporates vectors of application and inference of individuals. Language meaning is an aggregate of individual vectors of reference and inference based on vectors of respect individuals assign. That is the theory I propose, but the details need not be accepted to clarify the relationship between exemplar representation of individuals and social meaning. Exemplar representation functions in the use of language by supplying an exhibit to show us how to apply a word to refer to the objects of exemplar representation. This function in the usage of an individual may be corrected or overridden socially in terms of background information. The referential function of the exemplar remains a source of evidence, however fallible, and subject to correction that connects representation with the objects of linguistic and social reference. The exemplars may be private, they may be the conscious states of individuals, but their referential function remains a constituent that supplies, however fallibly and subject to revision, the connection between exemplar representation and the objects represented.

SUMMARY

Let us return to our simple example of Dante smelling the sensation to exhibit the structure of evidence and knowledge of the external world gained from the exemplarization of the sensation. There is a sensation that functions as a term of exemplar representation of sensations. This sensation exemplarization yields the truth security of the sensation of reflexive reference as the exemplar sensation functions to exhibit what the sensations represented are like. The exemplar is, of course, like itself, and, therefore, represents and refers to itself. As it refers to itself and is true of what it refers to, it is true of itself. We imagined that at first smell, Dante was unfamiliar with the smell of a skunk and lacked any conception of skunks. But the sensation called attention to itself and was exemplarized. Dante will not soon forget what the sensation was like.

However, the sensation will, perhaps at the same time, function to represent some quality in the external world, an odor out there. This quality exemplarization shows us that a sensation, when salient, may ambiguously represent a sensation and a quality in the external world functioning as an exemplar of what both the sensation and quality are like. This exemplarization yields knowledge of what the sensation is like and what the external quality is like. Exemplar representation yields a conception of represented items in terms of the way it exhibits what they are like. The exemplar is a functional constituent in the meaning or content of the conception. As a constituent of the meaning or content of the conception, it is evidence of the existence of the sensation and the external quality, showing the subject what they are like. There is more to the quality than the sensation Dante has; the quality will occasion the sensation in others and is, in fact, the spray of a skunk, though Dante does not initially know this. The quality out there, the external odor, is not reducible to sensations it occasions, but the sensation that Dante experiences is part and parcel, exhibit and representation, of how Dante conceives of the odor. The sensation, at this initial stage, is what the odor is like for Dante. It is his evidence that there is an odor out there in the external world. He knows from the evidence of sensation, an exemplarized term of representation, that there is an odor out there and something about what the odor is like, what it smells like, from the noxious sensation. The evidence for this knowledge is fallible like all evidence about external entities. The sensation could be produced by a device deceptively producing the sensation in his nose directly from some chemicals in his nose, or by more remote neurological stimulation producing the noxious sensation, leading Dante to think there is some external quality out there when there is not. In this case, the evidence of the exemplar is deceptive. However, even here, sensation exemplarization of the exemplar provides evidence and knowledge of the existence of the sensation. Whether it is possible to deceive Dante into thinking he has a sensation when he has none at all, I leave open, but in such a case sensation exemplarization would be missing and with it the evidence of exemplar representation. It is the presence of the exemplar and the exemplarization of it that yields evidence and knowledge of the existence of the sensation.

Beatrice intervenes and tells Dante that what he smells is a skunk. Before she tells him what skunks are like, he does not yet know much about what Beatrice means by the word "skunk." But if he replies, "So that is what a skunk smells like," part of what the term "skunk" means for Dante is acquired from the exemplar representations of the sensation and the quality of the odor. The exemplar representation has the functional role of identifying the meaning of "smell of a skunk" for Dante, exhibiting for him what that is like. As part of meaning, the exemplars are evidence for him of the application of the expression, "that is the smell of a skunk," or, more briefly, "skunk smell." He knows from the evidence of the exemplar what the smell of a skunk is like.

Beatrice then tells Dante, "A skunk is a small black animal with a divided white stripe down the back and a fluffy tail that sprays the noxious odor as a defense mechanism when threatened or injured." Now the meaning of the exemplar, and the sensation exemplarization of it, radiates to become part of the meaning, a quality exemplarization, of an external odor. Radiating wider, it becomes part of the meaning and object exemplarization for Dante of what the spray of a skunk is like as described by Beatrice. The exemplarized sensation, therefore, becomes evidence that a skunk nearby has sprayed. The sensation exemplarization is not infallible evidence that a skunk has sprayed, but the exemplarized sensation is part of what "spray of a skunk" means for Dante. It is his exhibit for what spray of a skunk smells like, and, therefore, evidence of the spray of a skunk. Dante knows what the spray of a skunk smells like in terms of his exemplarized sensation.

Dante's knowledge depends on accepting the authority and trustworthiness of Beatrice concerning what she tells him about the odor and skunks. He means what she means, and she means what we mean. That meaning is the social meaning of the words, the application of the word and the inferential network of the word in communal or aggregate use of the words. What more is required for Dante to know that what he smells is a skunk nearby?

To know that he smells a skunk from the evidence of the exemplar, he must be in a position in terms of his background system to answer objections to the claim that he smells a skunk. One objection is that Beatrice is not trustworthy in what she accepts and testifies about skunks. Another is that she is deceived in this instance about the smell. Another is that he is not trustworthy in evaluating the trustworthiness of Beatrice. Still another objection, more remote and metaphysical, is that the sensation is produced by deception. Dante, without reflecting on such considerations, is, I have imagined, in a position to defend his acceptance of the claim that he smells a skunk on the basis of the evidence of the exemplar sensation, which exhibits and represents the smell of a skunk, and in terms of his background information obtained from Beatrice. The evidence and background information are fallible. Dante might be deceived. But he trusts the evidence of his sense of smell and the background information supplied by Beatrice. He thinks he ought to trust them, that he is trustworthy in accepting them. Suppose, as I have in the example, that he is trustworthy in accepting and preferring to accept that what he does rather than the objections. Being trustworthy in accepting what he does and preferring to accept what he does, it is more reasonable for Dante to accept what he does than to accept the objections. That is what personally justifies him in accepting that he smells the spray of a skunk.

If he confronts a philosopher raising skeptical objections, he may reply that the sensation of smell and the premise of exemplar representation of it is evidence, which he can defend against objections, that personally justifies him in claiming he smells a skunk nearby. The defense of his claim would appeal to truths in his background system. Of course,

Dante need not reflect philosophically on his claim that he smells a skunk to know that he smells a skunk. It suffices that his background system supplies him with a personal justification and defense of a claim that he smells a skunk that is not defeated by errors in his background system. That is how Dante knows.

I have argued elsewhere (Lehrer, 2000b) for this conception of knowledge as personal justification of acceptance that is not defeated by errors in the background system of justification. Knowledge is undefeated personal justification. That is why Dante knows on the basis of the sensation of smell. The exemplarized sensation, radiating from sensation exemplarization, to quality exemplarization, and then to object exemplarization, is the premise of evidence because it is part of the meaning of the object claim, "That is what a skunk smells like!" The meaning of the claim is not exhausted by his sensation, of course, but that exemplarized sensation is part of the meaning of the object claim that gives Dante knowledge of the existence of an external quality, an odor, and an object, a skunk.

CONCLUSION AND QUALIFICATION

I conclude with a qualification concerning exemplar representation and a consideration of the application of the notion to our knowledge of the external world from other senses. The qualification is that I am not claiming that all sensations are exemplarized. Some sensations and other sensory stimuli may elicit representations of external things without being exemplarized when attention is not directed toward the character of the stimuli. This is often the case. I chose the example of Dante and the smell of the skunk because that obnoxious sensation directs attention to itself and is a plausible instance of unsophisticated exemplar representation. My claim about the exemplarization of this sensation is not intended to be a general cognitive science account about how all representations of external things arise from sensory stimuli. Dante is a special case, but as an epistemologist I am concerned with the philosophical problem of how one might justify the claim that one has defensible knowledge of the external world from premises representing the evidence of the senses. Exemplar representation of what the external world is like is sufficient for such defensible knowledge supported by undefeated justification. As one passes from genetic accounts about how our conceptions and beliefs of external things first arise in us to the epistemological question of what reasons we have to justify such conceptions and beliefs, exemplar representation supplies the answer. The epistemological role of exemplar representation may be extended to justify other perceptual claims. We may not at first attend to what the sensations and appearances are like when our conceptions and beliefs arise. They may be the transparent input of conception and belief. But when we take the philosophical turn in the quest for defensible knowledge and ask how such conceptions and beliefs may be justified, perhaps even to our philosophical selves who entertain reflective doubt that we have knowledge, exemplar representation supplies premises of justification. We may defend our claims by directing our attention to the sensations and appearances that we first passed over and exemplarize them. The exemplar representations provide us with premises to defend what we believe about the external world.

Why should we say that we know of the existence of external things on the basis of exemplars of sensory experience before we have exemplarized those experiences? There are many varieties of knowledge, but a salient form of knowledge in art and science, perhaps the most valuable, is the kind of knowledge that is defensible against objections. Defensibility is a capacity to meet objections that arise, even from internal doubts. The capacity to defend claims about the external world arises from the capacity to form exemplar representations of experience as evidence and reasons for accepting the existence of external things. This capacity to exemplarize experience, even when not yet exercised, is a basis of the defensibility of the target of knowledge.

The defense is that the exemplar exhibits what the object is like. The exemplar representation enables us to defend the claim that we perceive external objects, a skunk for example. Our defense runs in a familiar way. It smells like a skunk, it looks like a skunk, it feels like a skunk. It is a skunk. The defense involves the exemplarization of the smell, look, and feel, converting the stimuli, some of which may be initially transparent, into the opaque exemplar representations of the skunk. Exemplar representation gives us knowledge of what the sensory experiences are like and radiates out representationally becoming part of the meaning and evidence to defend accepting the claims about the external world. Exemplarization may not explain how all our conceptions of the external world arise, but it does explain how sensory experience can be converted to evidence and reasons in the justification game of defending what we accept. That capacity to convert experience into premises of evidence supplies us with defensible knowledge of the external world. We smell the truth.

3

KNOWLEDGE, AUTONOMY,

AND EXEMPLARS

REASONABLENESS AND TRUSTWORTHINESS ARGUMENT

There has been an ongoing perplexity about knowledge and autonomy. I approached the issue in earlier works (1997, 2000, 2016) when considering the role of trustworthiness of acceptance and preference in reasonableness, justification, and knowledge. I turn to an argument to explain how trustworthiness can sustain the reasonableness of acceptance, of preference for accepting one thing over another, and of reasoning from accepted premises.

My simple argument to explain reasonableness in terms of trustworthiness ran as follows:

> I am worthy of my trust in what I accept and prefer to accept in the pursuit of reason.
> I am trustworthy in what I accept and prefer to accept in the pursuit of reason.
> I am reasonable in what I accept and prefer to accept.

Knowledge requires more than reasonable acceptance. It requires personally justified acceptance that was irrefutable. My short account of what must be added to reasonableness to obtain justification is that one must be able to meet objections. An objection is met when it is more reasonable for the person to accept the target claim than the objection on the basis of his own background system of evaluation. The details get complicated, as I indicated earlier and in my previous work (Lehrer, 2000b). The basic idea is that if a person prefers accepting the target claim to the objection, and the person is reasonable in so preferring, then it is more reasonable for the person to accept the target claim than the objection. Of course, the evaluation system containing acceptances, preferences, and, I added, reasonings, will only yield knowledge if the justification does not depend on errors in the evaluation system that defeat the justification. The crux of the account is that trustworthiness of acceptances, preferences, and reasonings generates an evaluation system of reasonable and justified acceptances, which, when irrefutable by correction of errors in the system, yields knowledge. That is a short story about a complicated theory of knowledge. The word bite for the theory is as follows: Knowledge is undefeated and irrefutable justification. On this account, defeat and refutation are restricted to correction of errors in the background system. A critical feature is that it is a coherence theory because of the role of the evaluation system. However, coherence of a target claim with an evaluation system is a defense of the claim against objections. Thus, the coherence theory is an internal defensibility theory. Moreover, a principle of trustworthiness within the system supports the reasonableness of what one accepts, and it loops back through other acceptances onto the acceptance of itself, avoiding the need of an infinite regress Klein (2007) has defended or the need of a foundation that Chisholm (1966) defended. I call the principle of trustworthiness a *keystone*. The principle of trustworthiness has a similarity to principles of intellectual virtue articulated by Foley (2001), Sosa (2007), and Zagzebski (2012), which I noted in Lehrer (2001), as well as proper warrant (Plantinga, 1993). I insist, however, that trustworthiness is an overarching principle in the life of reason, rather than successful reliability discussed by Mattey (1989) in attaining some goal. It is a keystone loop at the top of the arches in the chapel of reason bracing the evaluation system into a coherent whole.

AUTONOMY, EXPLANATION, AND SELF-TRUST

How does the issue of autonomy enter into the account? Lack of autonomy is an objection to the claim that a person is worthy of his or her own trust. It is, therefore, an objection to the conclusion that a person is justified in accepting some target claim. Consider the notion of an objection. An objection to accepting a conclusion is a reason against accepting it. The objection might be met. A lack of autonomy in what you accept or prefer does not entail that you are not worthy of your trust. It is, however, a reason against thinking you are.

I gave an account of autonomy of preference (1997, 2004, 2016) indebted to, though differing from, the theory of higher order preference proposed by Frankfurt (1969). An autonomous preference is a preference in a preference structure concerning a specific option that you have because you prefer to have it. That preference for the preference structure I have called a *power preference*. The power preference is a preference for itself at the same time that it is a preference for other preferences in the structure. The primary explanation for the power preference must be the explanatory loop of that preference back onto itself. That is what insures autonomy and freedom of choice. The explanatory loop explains the way in which I am the autonomous agent of my power preference. I have that preference as the primary explanation of why I prefer to have it. There may be further causes of the power preference, but they are secondary. The causal order of nature is in this way compatible with the autonomy of the power preference.

Moreover, there is a special power preference, which I call an *ultrapreference*, that is a preference for choosing according to a specific system of reasons. Your reasons for choosing an option are the reasons you prefer to guide or support your choice. It is important to think of the ultrapreference as a power preference that you have because you prefer to have it. The power preference loops back onto itself as you prefer the system of reasons that guide or support your preferences because you prefer that system of reasons. It is important to notice that the power preference for the choice of action or acceptance may occur at the same time as the choice of the ultrapreference for the system of reasons that support the choice of action or acceptance. It is natural to think of appealing to an antecedent system of reasoning to guide choice, but some of our most important preferences, life-altering and revolutionary scientific preferences, occur in response to sudden experiences of insight and conversion that realize a power preference of choice and an ultrapreference of reasoning at the same time. Once again, when the ultrapreference and the power preference are the primary explanation of why we have them in an explanatory loop, they exhibit our autonomy in causal order.

The principles of trustworthiness and the power preference both contain a loop that makes them self-supporting, revealing how they illuminate knowledge and autonomy. They are not independent of other support, though they support themselves. Our trustworthiness depends on what we accept, as it makes us reasonable in what we accept. Our power preference depends on our preferences as it makes us autonomous in our preferences. It is the primacy of the explanatory loop that makes causal influences upon us compatible with our reasonableness and autonomy. Self-sustenance may depend on what is available to sustain us, in preference and acceptance. At the same time it remains primary in explanation.

THEORIES OF KNOWLEDGE

There are widely opposed theories of knowledge I wish to argue can be tied together in a loop of sustained autonomy. Some theories of knowledge, along with views of mentality in general, focus on those representational responses that are automatic or modular. I will not tie this to any particular account. Dretske (1981, 1995) and Fodor (1983) give us different accounts of representation and first-level belief but neither account appears to have anything to do with autonomy. So these accounts, with their emphasis on first-level systems of automatic response of mechanical information processing systems, however conceived specifically, argue for a level of representation, belief, and, in the case of Dretske, knowledge, that does not involve higher level evaluation or autonomous reflection.

Fodor (1983) suggested a level of response beyond the output of a modular input system. The representational output of the input system was itself input for a central system with access to background information. This opens the door to the entrance of autonomy at the level of central system processing. But what is the connection between first-level, automatic, perhaps even encapsulated representational response, if Fodor is right, and the account I suggested above that gives a large role to autonomy? What is the role of autonomy in representation beyond the level of automatic or modular response?

Some levels of perceptual response are modular or at least so driven by habit as to be irresistible. There is some automatic and irresistible output of representation in response to a stimulus. The output of representation of some object before me, a chair for example, leads beyond representation to a doxastic state, a belief that there is a chair before me. The practical affairs of life and the need to deal with the hazards and opportunities thereof create the need to add a doxastic aspect, belief, to the impressions of sense. At early stages of life such beliefs are beyond question and doubt. The young child believes both the representations of experience and the representations of others without an understanding of the distinction between truth and error. It is helplessly gullible, as Reid ([1785] 1983) noted, and does not understand deception at this stage.

BEYOND BELIEF TO ACCEPTANCE

The need for evaluation confronts original belief as we mature. We then discover that we can be deceived by experience and by others. We develop a capacity to evaluate the representations of sense, memory, and testimony as we come to distinguish truth from error. When the capacity for evaluation and discrimination of truth from error is activated, we can reflect on the impressions and beliefs we have, rejecting some and accepting others. Thus, I have argued, with others, that it is important to distinguish between the state of belief, which usually arises without our choosing and may remain contrary to our will, and more autonomous evaluation of the belief leading to acceptance or rejection of the belief. The fixation and resilience of belief is a constraint on our cognitive autonomy. However, the evaluation of belief, whether resulting in acceptance or rejection of it, opens a new chapter of representation, and, with it, a new level of autonomous representation, preference, and acceptance.

Consider an example of the evaluation of belief. It may occur to me as I have a visual impression of chair in front of me that convinces me the chair exists, that I am in a deceptive environment, a place of illusion. So maybe what looks like a chair before me is a brilliant illusion produced by mirrors or holograms. I reach where I see it and, feeling nothing, reject the impression. Sense may be by sense corrected, as Hobbes suggested, but only with the assistance of a background system. For my lack of feeling a chair may be the result of another illusion, for example, tactile numbness. Reflection calls on a system of information for an answer to the question of the presence of the chair, leading me to place my trust in myself to decide what to accept and reject. Here I confront my autonomy. It is up to me to decide to accept, reject, or suspend judgment on my impression of the presence of the chair. In judging, I confront choice, and in choice, I confront self-trust. I must trust myself in order to proceed, and in so doing consider myself worthy of my trust. We have returned to the argument we ran at the beginning. It leads me from acceptance and my trustworthiness in what I accept to the reasonableness of acceptance.

It is important to notice that my acceptance of my being trustworthy in what I accept does not entail that I am trustworthy in what I accept. Having noticed the possibility of deception, I recognize that I am fallible, and, being fallible about what I accept, I must recognize that I am fallible in accepting that I am trustworthy in what I accept as well as other matters. There is systematic support for my thinking that I am trustworthy in what I accept. However, my trustworthiness in accepting the items of that system depends for support on my being correct in accepting that I am trustworthy in accepting those items. There is a small loop of my acceptance of my trustworthiness back onto itself supported, at the same time, by a greater loop of what I accept and the trustworthiness of accepting it. Is there a foundation in the principle of trustworthiness for the other things I accept, or a bootstrapping of the principle itself from the system of acceptances? The metaphors are misleading because they are unidirectional. There is mutual support, like a looping keystone in a system of arches in a chapel.

The advantage of the loop of trustworthiness is that it is explanatory. To explain something to my satisfaction, I must accept it, but it must also be true. So the principle of trustworthiness contained in the system of things I accept explains why I am trustworthy in accepting it, when I am, indeed, trustworthy. It explains my trustworthiness in the other things I accept, leading me to the acceptance of my trustworthiness itself. Another metaphor, suggested by Reid ([1785] 1983), for the relationship between individual acceptances and the general principle, is that of light. Reid remarked that light is like evidence in that as light reveals the illuminated objects, it also reveals itself. My preference for the keystone metaphor is that it includes a model of mutual support. Of course, the illuminated object reflects the light as well, and thus both light and keystone are appropriate metaphors.

As we proceed from consideration of a level of representation and belief that may be irresistible, as Reid suggested, to a level of acceptance that is autonomous, it is important to remember that belief considered as a dispositional or functional state has a resilience that resists the efforts of the autonomous evaluation. I am not claiming that the negative evaluation of a belief has no causal influence on the sustenance of it, but the manner of influence is complex and uncertain. People find themselves continuing to believe what reflection and additional information leads them to consider an error, and such sustenance is even more readily noted by others when someone later espouses a view they had admitted in conversation to be erroneous. This may be politeness or duplicity, but that should not be assumed. Some people may evaluate a belief negatively and find, perhaps to their own chagrin, that they later act as though they believe it. One only needs to consider the beliefs of prejudice to find such instances in oneself. Belief does not transform itself immediately to match the results of evaluation and reflection. Perhaps there is some advantage to having a system that responds automatically and unreflectively to accompany another system of evaluation and autonomy. Automaticity may ground autonomy.

I have noted the similarity between belief and evaluated acceptance, on the one hand, and desire and evaluated preference, on the other. I may evaluate a desire negatively and prefer not to satisfy it. Desire is resilient, however, like belief, and does not immediately disappear when evaluated negatively. A similar distinction exists between automatic inference and evaluated reasoning, for we may continue to draw inferences we have evaluated as fallacious. My argument is and was (Lehrer, 1997, 2000b) that there is a level of evaluation of representation of belief, desire, and inference that is autonomous. At that level, we evaluate these states to arrive at evaluated acceptance, evaluated preference, and evaluated reasoning. This level of evaluation does not automatically amend the original beliefs, desires, or inferences. In some cases, this may seem distressing. However, the common sense answer from Reid ([1785] 1983) to Hume (1888), whom he construed as a skeptic, was that there may be some advantage in continuing to believe what is irresistible—the existence of an external world, for example—even when we make war with these beliefs in philosophical reflection. Irresistible representation may provide a common-sense constraint on ratiocination.

AUTONOMY AND REPRESENTATION

To further explore the role of autonomy in representation, let us return to the level of sensory output response. Such output responses may not be representations of what the stimulus itself is like. For example, a visual sensation may elicit a representation of an external moving object without representing what the sensation is like. At other times, a stimulus may elicit a representation of what a sensation is like, a stinking smell, of the spray of a skunk that we noted in Chapter 2, without providing a representation of the external object that provides the sensation. It is natural in the second kind of case to say that the person knows what the sensation is like from the sensory experience alone while initially ignorant of the cause. When the person considers what is causing the sensation, interpretation, autonomy, and reasoning may enter into what the person accepts. But we may have knowledge of what a sensation is like without an exercise of reason or autonomy. This knowledge of the sensation of smell may elicit an interpretation of the presence of an external object, a skunk. That interpretation, further explained in Chapter 2, is chosen by the subject, who is the agent of the representation.

Such simple examples lead us into issues of the way in which we exercise our autonomy to represent the objects of our world and, at the same time, to represent what we are like. We are exercising our autonomy representing our world and ourselves, ourselves in the world, and the world in ourselves. My claim previously discussed here and in (Lehrer, 2011) is that there is a special kind of representation in terms of experience, exemplar representation, using the experience as an exemplar to exhibit what something is like. There is a Janus-faced character to experience used as exemplars—for example, appearances, sensations, and impressions—as we use them to show us what some external thing is like, perhaps some physical object or theoretical entity. Yet, at the same time, the exemplars we use to represent those things show us how we conceive of what the things are like in terms of the exemplars of our experience, those appearances, sensations, and impressions. The experience taken as an exemplar representation, when attention is directed toward what it is like in itself, which I call *aesthetic attention* because of the salience of it in the aesthetic appreciation, faces in two directions, like Janus. The exemplar faces outward toward the world, to show us what it is like for us, and also in the other direction, inward toward the mind, to show us what we are like representing what the world is like. The exemplar, used like a sample, functions as a term of reference, standing for the things it represents as it shows us what they are all like, namely, the exemplar. This account is indebted to Goodman's (1968, 1978) account of exemplification, but differs from it in taking the exemplar itself as a term used to refer to the individuals to which it applies. For Goodman, the sample refers to a property or predicate exemplified by the sample, while in my view, Lehrer (2006, 2011), the exemplar refers directly to itself reflexively as well as to the other members of the class of individuals represented by it, taking on the role of a predicate. I shall explain how the exemplar takes on this role in Chapter 4.

I propose, as I have argued, that this solves the problem of the representation of the external world, what it is like, and of the internal world, what we are like. A simple sensation, a smell, is a sign of some external quality that is the source of sensation and, at the same time, of how we think of the external quality, in terms of the sensation that marks that quality in conceptual space. This Janus attention and exemplar use of sensory experience shows us what Wittgenstein ([1922] 1999) said could not be fully described but only be shown, namely, what the form of representation and intentionality are like. This leaves a question about reason, justification, and knowledge unanswered. It is, of course, one thing to represent the world in a certain way, and it is another thing to be reasonable and justified in accepting the representation in a way that leads to knowledge. So how do we get from representation, even exemplar representation, to epistemology, to a justified claim to truth?

REPRESENTATION AND JUSTIFICATION

Reasonableness and justification have truth as an epistemological objective if for no other reason than that truth is a condition of knowledge. We may say that we know when we lack truth, but we are wrong in claiming the prize of knowledge without capturing truth. "Know" is a success word, and a minimal condition for success in knowing is that we be right, that is, that what we claim is true. Note that exemplar representation, when the exemplar is used as an exhibit to pick out what it refers to, loops reflexively back onto itself as one of the things to which it refers. If we use our experience of an untitled painting in monochrome pink, a gorgeous painting *Pink Square* by Olivier Mosset (1990), as an exemplar exhibiting what experience of a special color of pink is like, the exemplar becomes a term of reference, and the experience used as the exemplar representation refers to itself as well as to the other things it represents. We say that an exemplar term of reference, like a predicate, is true of things, of an experience, a color, a paint, or an artwork. The exemplar taken as an exhibit is used as a term of reference. It is true of things to which it refers, including, of course, reflexively itself. There is a safe loop of truth of the exhibit back onto itself as one of those things it exhibits. This is not a logical guarantee, however, for it rests on a representational or cognitive activity of using one thing to stand for another, and such activities, if naturally functioning to generate a truth loop, can function in other ways, or simply dysfunction and fail to secure the loop.

UNDEFEATED JUSTIFICATION AND EXEMPLAR REPRESENTATION

What is the connection between exemplar representation and undefeated or irrefutable justification? Exemplar representation, though it contains a loop back onto itself as an exemplarization of itself, extends representationally beyond experiences to other things to which they refer. A term of representation is ambiguous. Consider the experience of pink in front of the Mosset monochrome. The exemplar experience picks out a kind of color experience to which it refers. At the same time, reference extends beyond experience representationally. The exemplar shows us what a kind of experience is like, and, at the same time, the exemplar shows us what a painting is like. Moreover, the exemplar reaches referentially beyond the painting and paint as we attach affective expression to the exemplar. It shows us the prettiness of pink. The figurative emptiness of the painting immerses us in pink, into the pleasure of being in the pink. The exemplar refers beyond color to a mood of feeling good. The associations multiply to sound and the sky. So what am I justified in accepting? That the experience refers as an exemplar to a class of experiences of a kind it exhibits and beyond the experiences to other things. The tight truth loop of the exemplar onto itself is lost as reference extends beyond itself, and the expansion of representation to an artwork, to paint, to feelings of being in the pink, are part of a distinction in conceptual space marked by the exemplar for me. I use it to mark the distinction, for example, between the pink monochrome and other monochromes in Mosset 6 as well as other artworks.

Ben Vautier (1975) shows us by writing words in color the difference between exemplar representation and verbal representation even when the exemplar is itself a word. Consider the word "red" written in ordinary black type. It is a predicate referring to red things. Now, imitating Vautier, consider the word in colored red like the word "this" in Figure 1.

Red

is

a

word

One is aware of a double mode of reference of the word colored red. It not only refers to red things, but also shows us what they are like. So the exemplar experience, like the word in black, refers to red things, but unlike the word in black, shows us what they are like. It functions as a referring term applying to itself as well as to other things.

How much do I know about the exemplar? I know what my experience of it is like, and this is a form of propositional content as the exemplar functions as a referring term that may be used cognitively like a predicate. The exemplar does double service, reflexively becoming a general term that first applies to itself and then to other things. There are objections, of course, to what I accept about this representation as well as any other, namely, that I am making some mistake even in applying the term to itself. I accept that I am not making such a mistake and that I should trust myself in how I represent the exemplar in terms of itself. I know what it is like up to that limit with as much certainty as the use of my faculties allows. Going beyond the immediacy of experience, I accept that the exemplar is an appearance of a work of art hanging on the wall. I could be wrong; I can always be deceived when I use an exemplar of experience to represent an external object, and, of course, art museums play on deception. I could be deceived.

It is more reasonable in this instance to accept that I am not deceived, and my preference for accepting that the exemplar shows me what an artwork is like trumps the objection that I am deceived. The trump card is my self-trust and my being worthy of it. I must be trustworthy in what I accept in these matters or my justification is defeated by an error about my trustworthiness. This is not an appeal to status. It is not an appeal to what Danto (1964, 1994), and Dickie (1974) following him, calls the artworld. It is instead an appeal to the exemplar. There is an experience—it takes me into color, into feeling of being in the pink—in a way that adds value to experience. It is my experience that convinces me it is an artwork, not the distinguished members of the artworld, however much I value their capacity to show me what I do not know.

I have fixed on art, but science would do as well. The words "I am in the pink" are themselves enticing, but the content of the expression has to be filled in, as Isenberg (1949) insisted long ago, by experience. Much the same is true of scientific discourse. The discourse may delight us as it stimulates the imagination, but experience has to fill in the content of discourse or the discourse remains disconnected from reality. String theory is a delightful story about the relation between particles and waves, and mathematically brilliant as well, but the content of the theory has to be filled in by experience that tests the mettle of the theory. I am making a point beyond what has been made by the multitude who insist on the importance of operationalizing theory. It is that the content or meaning of theory depends on the content or meaning of some experience, an exemplar representation of content that exhibits that content or meaning by being a constituent of it. The exemplar is part and parcel, exhibit and representation, of the content or meaning. It is representation that contains itself as the experience represented. When exemplar representation is added to the theory, to the content of theoretical discourse, the experienced exemplar exhibiting what it is like extends the experience into the meaning of the world of theory it describes. Adding exemplar representation to the theoretical content or meaning of the description of the world exhibits what cannot be described about the connection between experience and theory.

LINGUISTIC DESCRIPTION AND REPRESENTATIONAL THEORY: A HISTORICAL NOTE

To fully understand the relationship between exemplar representation and linguistic description, it is essential to note some history of representational theory about the connection between sensory experience and forms of representation. To explain the evidential justification relation between sensory experiences and descriptions of external objects, both perceptual objects such as chairs and theoretical objects such as electrons, some philosophers, most notably phenomenalists, Ayer (1940) and Lewis (1946), attempted an explanation in terms of relations between linguistic descriptions of sensory experiences and linguistic descriptions of external objects. Rorty (1967) appropriately called this the *linguistic turn*, because it was an attempt to explain the relations of evidence and justification in terms of language. One form of explanation consisted of an attempted reduction of descriptions of external objects to descriptions of sensory experiences, either descriptions of what we actually experience or would experience if we perceived the external objects. This form of explanation was often a two-tier reduction. The first tier was the reduction of descriptions of perceptual objects to lower-level descriptions of sensory experience, and the second tier was the reduction of descriptions of theoretical objects to descriptions of perceptual objects. It was notable that the program failed because reductions at both levels failed. The reason in both cases was that there were features of external objects that transcended the features that could be described at the lower level. What a perceptual object could reveal in sensory experience was of infinite variety depending on objective conditions of surrounding circumstances and the condition of the perceiver. The role of infinity in the failure of reduction of theoretical objects to perceptual objects was more notable, as Hempel (1965) pointed out. Theoretical description is explicitly mathematical and allows for an infinity of values while observation, that is, perception, is finitely limited in powers of discrimination. The infinite values of mathematically articulated theoretical description could not be reduced to the finite values of observation description.

However, the failure of reduction did not exclude the possibility that there were relations of meaning, *meaning postulates* as Hempel called them, relating the meaning of descriptions of items at one level to items at another level, even if such postulates did not exhaust the meaning of descriptions at a higher level. It might be a matter of meaning that perceptual description is semantically connected with sensory description and that theoretical description is semantically connected with perceptual description even though one level of description is not reducible to the lower level. The details of the semantic connection, the connection of meaning, are not our present concern, though, as I shall propose in Chapter 4, the connection may be stochastic or probabilistic, as Lewis (1946) argued earlier. There was, however, a deeper problem in the linguistic turn.

The fundamental problem, and one I previously neglected to notice, was the problem of providing a theory of meaning that connected descriptive language with the experience of the world, whether the world of perceptual objects or theoretical objects, that explained how sensory experience could provide evidence for the existence of such objects. The first step was to explain the semantic description between words and experience. Schlick (1979), Ayer (1940), and Lewis (1946) attempted to provide some connection between words and experiences that would provide an infallible or incorrigible link between words and experiences. A favorite strategy was to begin with demonstratives. I will not here trace the discussion of these efforts. The basic problem was that purely demonstrative uses of language do not convey the information about what the experience is like that is needed to formulate a premise of evidence about what the experience is like. Discourse that does not tell us anything about what our experience of the world is like cannot explain how such discourse provides evidence for even the existence of sensory experience, much less for the existence of an external world. It lacks the informative content of experience necessary to convert the discourse to evidence. There is an explanatory gap between language and the sensory experience it is meant to represent.

Moreover, the explanatory gap becomes a truth gap. Ayer and Lewis sought to articulate a semantics for a language describing sensory experiences, a sense data language, that was incorrigible and in that way closed the truth gap. But descriptors and the experiences are distinct from one another, and, as a result, the use of the descriptors to describe experience can fail to be correct just because the meaning of the descriptors is distinct from what they describe. There is no way to close the explanatory and semantic gap between language and what it describes. The history of skeptical hypotheses about evil demons and brains in vats can be extended to include demonic and neurological deception about the use of discourse to describe our sensory experiences themselves as well as deception about the external world. Powerful mischief makers could lead us to report we are in pain when not in pain, that we experience appearances when we do not, by altering how we use the discourse. We can be deceived because of a cleft at the heart of meaning between our language and our world. The gap between words and experiences cannot be closed by appeal to some infallible use of language. The meaning of language cannot make us infallible in our employment of it, for, simply put, we are fallible in our application of language to something beyond it.

The foregoing is controversial, as philosophy with substance must be, but the history of twentieth-century philosophy supports it. Sellars (1963a) and Quine (1960) attempted to secure a functional connection of meaning with experience by offering stimulus-response connection as the explanation of how our use of language, and in the former case, the meaning of language, is connected to the world outside language. They conceded and insisted on the fallibility and corrigibility of our use of language, as the same words may be functionally related in a diverse ways to experience and the world beyond it. Moreover, we may be ignorant of how our words are functionally related to other things, including our own sensory experiences, and, therefore, ignorant of the meaning of our descriptions of our sensations and sensory states. Meaning becomes a matter of correlation, on some accounts resulting from conditioning, on other accounts in other ways. But we may be totally ignorant, totally unaware, of what the correlation is like.

I do not wish to argue against such theories as contributions to a theory of meaning. It is clear as both Reid (1863) and much later Putnam (1975) argued that we sometimes use language when we mean what some specialist, a lawyer or scientist, means without knowing what they mean. But we cannot totally fail to know what the connection is like between our representation of experience and the experience represented to avoid the disconnection and isolation of representation to what it represents. Something is missing in linguistic theorizing that is needed to close the explanatory and semantic gap between our representation of our experience of the world and linguistic description. What is missing is a form of representation beyond language that supplies a transparent connection between representation and experience. That connection is the exemplar representation of experience that provides us with knowledge of what the connection is like.

In exemplarization of experience, we have an explanation of what the connection is like as soon as we direct our attention to what our sensory experiences are like. For we know what the experiences are like when we attend to them whether we can find a linguistic description or not. As described in Chapter 2, Dante knows what his sensation of smell is like before he knows that it is caused by the spray of a skunk. He may find words inadequate to describe what his sensory experience is like, but he knows what it is like. His knowledge, like all knowledge, involves some conception of what it is like, even though he can find no words to express his conception. Noticing this provides us a solution to the problem of connecting representation and experience that empiricists have sought. The solution is the theory of exemplarization, of using the experience itself to represent itself as well as other things beyond it and what words can describe. The explanatory gap and the truth gap are closed by the identity of the exemplar with what it represents, namely, the exemplar itself. As we know what the exemplar is like, we know, at the same time, what the exemplar representation of the experience is like. Finally, as we join exemplar representation with linguistic description of our experience of the world, we obtain the semantic connection, the connection of meaning and truth, from the transparency of exemplar representation.

TRUTH AND SELF-TRUST

We have to find some security in the representation of the world and ourselves in our autonomous acceptance of what we in our world are like and what our world in us is like. The way in which our world is in us is revealed in the Janus-faced exemplar when we confront our autonomy. We have to choose the meaning of art, theory, and discourse, and that autonomous choice connects us with the world. That is how the coherent and systematic story can contain, as Quine (1969) suggested, its own theory of truth. Theory and the truth of it are joined to produce justification undefeated and unrefuted by error. Knowledge is attained. We exercise our autonomy in the way that we take exemplars from experience to construct the conditions of truth. The loop of exemplarization connects theory and experience, putting theory to the test of experience. Remember, however much I have said, that the way in which experience is connected by exemplarization with representation is something that can only be shown. Talk is the game of philosophy. The rules of the game depend on a form of representation that ties our discourse together with our world. The tie is exemplarization. It exhibits the way that the form of representation transcends what can be said. That is where truth comes from. It is what makes us worthy of our trust as we autonomously exemplarize our experience of our world in ourselves.

4

EXEMPLARS, TRUTH, AND
SCIENTIFIC REVOLUTION

FORMS OF EXEMPLAR
REPRESENTATION: OSTENSIVE

I return in this chapter to the narrative from which I began. I began insisting on the importance of justification interpreted as a form of defensibility in terms of a background system. Justification is a form of local coherence with a background evaluation system. I argued that undefeated and irrefutable defensibility is knowledge because of the relation to truth in an ultrasystem. That system is the residue of the evaluation system when error is removed. I turned to an account of exemplar representation as an account of meaning and evidence of truth. Here I seek to connect the account of exemplar representation with truth and knowledge. My intention is to explain the way in which exemplar representation provides the empirical connection of undefeated and irrefutable defensibility. To accomplish, this I shall now refine and expand the theory of exemplar representation.

I return to the notion of exemplar representation. An exemplar representing a class of objects refers to those objects and is true of those objects when the exemplar representation is ostensive, that is, when the exemplar is used to stand for a class of experiences as an exhibit of what the experiences are like. Ostensive exemplar representation of an individual sensory experience results from several operations, not necessarily in any temporal sequence. The first is distinguishing the individual from other individuals in the environment. Reid (1863) called this *abstraction*. It is the focusing of attention in a way that distinguishes an individual that may be used as an exhibit of a class of individuals. The second is generalization of the individual to stand for a class of individuals it is used to represent. In this operation, the exemplar functions as an exhibit to show us what the represented individuals are like, marking a distinction between members of the class it represents and those not in the class. At this stage of exemplarization, the exemplar acquires representational meaning. It is a symbol representing a class of objects of which it is a member. It is both a vehicle of representation and one of the things it reflexively represents.

I have claimed that the exemplar representation is true of the objects it represents, including itself, and provides us with an experience of what the truth connection between a representation and what it represents is like. Some have objected that, though the exemplar may stand for or represent other experiences, it is not true of those experiences. I have compared the use of the exemplar with that of a sample used to represent a class. The objection is that, although a sample may stand for a class of objects of which it is a sample, it is not true of those objects. There is some intuitive plausibility in this objection that demands that I make explicit another operation. The operations of abstraction and generalization, even including marking a distinction between what is represented and what is not, do not yet include the addition of the formal feature of being used like a predicate. Abstraction and generalization do not entail that the exemplar is true of the objects it stands for because it may lack the formal feature of a predicate that can be affirmed of a subject.

I now wish to make explicit that in ostensive exemplarization the exemplar is used to function as a predicate representing the exemplarized class. This is the third operation involved in ostensive exemplarization of an individual experience. The operations are the direction of attention to an individual to be used as an exemplar, generalization from the exemplar to be used as an exhibit of a represented class, and, finally, assignment of the formal role of a predicate affirmed of the members of the represented class. Having acquired the role of a predicate affirmed of the represented objects, it acquires the formal role of referring to the objects of which it is affirmed and to which it applies. The exemplar predicate is true of the objects to which it refers. The exemplar predicate, which is an exemplar representation, shows us what the truth connection is like as it is reflexively true of itself.

There is a problem about speaking of the addition of a predicative role to the exemplar. Many will think of a predicate as a word in a conventional language, English for example. That is not my intention when I say that the exemplar is used as a predicate. The competence to understand the formal structure of subject and predicate, of a predicate affirmed of subject, precedes and is a necessary condition of the acquisition of conventional language, including the words and their grammatical role. This understanding of formal structure may be innate. The predicative role of exemplar representation may be acquired from innate understanding of the role of a predicate as something affirmed of an object without the association with a predicate in a conventional language. Moreover, there may be no predicate in a conventional language that refers to the same class of experiences represented by the exemplar. How we exemplarize may be influenced by a multiplicity of background factors, which may fail to include the association of the exemplar with a word in any conventional language, as I explained in Chapter 3.

It is notable that both Hume (1888) in the eighteenth century as well Goodman (1968) in the twentieth century construed the understanding of the predicate role of the experience as the result of the association with a word in a natural language. Such association may often occur, but it is clear that we may recognize a quality of experience we predicate of something in thought before we can find words to describe the quality. Moreover, words might fail to capture the character of what we know the experience is like as we represent it to ourselves. Exemplar representation, exemplar predication, captures that character of what the experience is like. The exemplarized representation is a predicate in thought affirmed of a subject. It is a component in thought and, in that way, in the language of thought that is distinct from conventional language.

EXEMPLARS AND WORDS

However, the exemplar predicate may pick out the same class of things as some predicate in a conventional language by serving to exhibit what the things referred to by the word are like. In that way, the exemplar representation becomes attached to the meaning of a word and determines how we apply the word. I shall return to the subject of attaching exemplar representations to words to connect words with experience. Here I note, for the purpose of clarifying how an exemplar can function like a predicate, that an exemplar acting as a sample can at the same time stand in for a predicative word in a language. The initial oddity of thinking of a sample as true of the members of the class of things it represents may be the lack of a conventional place for such items in a subject and predicate structure. However, the sample can, in addition to its role as an exemplar, sample, or paradigm, stand in for a predicate. Consider the sentence in English in Figure 1.

Now compare this to the sentence in which the word "this" is not in red:

R. My red color sensation is like this.

The color of the demonstrative in Figure 1 exhibits what the experienced sensation is like, unlike in R above, and the experience of it becomes an exemplar representation of what it is like. The experience of how the word looks shows you what an experience of the sensation is like and stands for experiences of such sensations. The word "this," occurring in color in Figure 1, exhibits what the sensations are like, adding content to the demonstrative reference. The word refers to what a sensation is like and, because of the color of the word, exhibits what it is like. The sensation of the color of the word shows us what the sensation is like at the same time that it refers to the sensation. Moreover, the colored word in Figure 1 is true of itself because of the exemplarized sensation. However, it is not simply the word "this" in Figure 1, but the exemplarized sensation that is converted to a predicate that is true of itself. We experience the sensation as an

Figure 1

My color sensation is like

this

exhibit of what the sensation referred to is like. That creates the reflexive reference of the exemplar back onto itself as the exemplar stands in for a predicate referring to itself. I shall call this predicative use of the experience *ostensive exemplar predication*. It is the same as sensation exemplarization but with the predicative role made explicit. The ostensive exemplar predicate refers to itself, is predicated of itself, and is true of itself as well as other sensations.

Note that ostensive predication already uses the exemplar to refer to something beyond itself, revealing its intentionality. It refers to other sensations as it represents them, exhibiting what they are like. That opens the possibility of using the exemplar to exhibit what things other than sensations are like. In the example in Figure 1, the red color of "this" exhibits what a color is like. Part of our conception of what colors are like is based on our sensations of color. The color and the meaning of the color word "red" is not reducible to sensations or experiences. The color of an object may persist unexperienced, but the sensations, the sensation of the color, remains, as Reid suggested, (1863) a capital part of the meaning of color words, that is, of how we conceive of color. Moreover, as the use of color samples of paint to represent paint illustrates, our sensations of the sample are a capital part of the meaning of color words and how we conceive of colors.

INFERENTIAL EXEMPLAR REPRESENTATION

We have noted that ostensive exemplar representation already has the intentionality of referring to other experiences it represents. This may lead one to infer the existence of other represented experiences from the exemplar, for example, later experiences of the sensation of "this" as one returns to Figure 1. Moreover, the exemplar representation may extend to the representation of objects beyond sensations, the external objects of colored letters in a text and paint in a can. Ostensive exemplar representations may become part of the meaning of our representation of external objects. They may be used to exhibit what the external objects are like, or, more cautiously, to what our experiences of them are like to us. The exemplarization of a look, feel, and smell may become part of our representation of how a duck looks, feels, and smells. These exemplar representations may also become attached to the meaning of the word "duck" functioning to guide our application of the word. Attaching the exemplar representation to words greatly enriches the inferential structure of the exemplar representation.

The conclusion is that exemplar representation radiates from the exemplarized experience to objects in the external world as they become attached to the meaning of the words exhibiting how our experience is connected to the world we describe. As the exemplar representations become attached to the meaning of words we use to describe the world, the exemplars we experience become premises for inferring the existence of the objects and events of our world. We thus add inferential predicative exemplarization to ostensive predicative exemplarization. Inferential predicative exemplarization will include the exemplarization of external qualities, quality exemplarization, as well as the exemplarization of external objects, object exemplarization.

EXEMPLARS AS EVIDENCE OF THE EXTERNAL WORLD

These forms of exemplar representation involve several operations or functions that again might not occur sequentially. First of all, the sensory exemplars in inferential predicative exemplarization are exemplar representations exhibiting what it is like to experience the external objects represented by them. Secondly, the exemplar functions in inferential predicative exemplarization as a sign of the existence of the external object. Thirdly, the exemplar functions as a predicate in a premise for inferring the existence of the external object. In both ostensive predicative exemplarization and inferential predicative exemplarization, the sensory exemplar is attached to the content or meaning of the exemplar representation and the associated word in order to exhibit what the represented object is like. The exemplar thus shows us how to apply the exemplar representation and the associated word. In both ostensive and inferential predicative exemplarization, the exemplar functions as both the term of representation and part of the content or meaning of the representation.

However, it is important to notice that in inferential exemplar representation of the external world, the sensory exemplar that reflexively represents itself also represents objects beyond itself that have properties that are unlike sensory qualia of the exemplar. Persistence in time and space, even when not experienced, and other transcendent properties of external objects go beyond our experience of the sensory exemplars. Nevertheless, the exemplar, exemplarized as an inferential predicate, remains evidence of the existence of the external object containing those properties.

EXEMPLAR REPRESENTATION AND AUTONOMY

As we consider the functional role of exemplar representations in meaning and application of predicates, whether in language of thought or social discourse, we confront our autonomy in how we use experience to represent the world as we noted in Chapter 3. For example, to return to our example of the smell of a skunk used to represent a skunk discussed in Chapter 2, we note that our original experience of the offensive odor may leave us with an unattached exemplar representation of a sensation. We may attach the exemplar representation of the sensation initially to some unknown external source and think of the sensation as emanating from it. At this point we think, and know, that something stinks. We have some conception of the external source in terms of the functional role of an exemplar representing it. We also have evidence from the exemplar representation that something out there stinks. There is a smell out there. We also confront our fallibility since there is the possibility that the sensation is the result of some internal olfactory abnormality. The objection that sensation is such a deceptive result is one that may be met in terms of our background system. In that system we autonomously prefer accepting that the sensation is externally caused to the hypothesis, which may not even occur to us, that the sensation is the result of olfactory abnormality. We accept the externality of the stink, and it is more reasonable for us on our background system, our evaluation system, to accept that something external to us stinks than to accept that our sensation is the result of olfactory abnormality. With objections met by our evaluation system and the defense sustained in our ultrasystem, we may know from the evidence of the exemplar representation that something external to us stinks. Our representation of something external that stinks, as well as our acceptance and defense of it, are a matter of choice, however unreflective, and exhibit our representational and epistemic autonomy.

It is important to take note of our choice in how we attach exemplar representation to an external object. As the story in Chapter 2 proceeds, Dante is told by someone he considers trustworthy, namely Beatrice, that the odor is caused by the secretion of an animal, a skunk. At this point in the story, the exemplar representation is attached to a descriptor in language, and it is considered to be the smell of a skunk. The exemplar represented something external to Dante, and now it represents a skunk. Attaching the exemplar representation to an external cause and then a skunk reflects an autonomous preference for using the exemplar to represent sensations, an external cause, and, finally, a skunk. Dante, or we instead if we replace Dante with ourselves in the scenario, may believe all these things spontaneously. But our acceptance of our exemplar representation of what the experience is like, a kind of sensation, an external smell, and, finally, a skunk, reflects our autonomous evaluation of these matters and becomes part of our evaluation system. That the acceptance, if not the belief, is a matter of choice is revealed by the rejection of what is believed by a total skeptic. The total skeptic, as Reid (1863) and Hume (1888) agreed, might not be able to cast off his natural beliefs as a result of his skeptical machinations. But, I suggest, he may evaluate these beliefs negatively and prefer not to accept them. Beliefs may be irresistible, but our evaluation of them reflects our autonomy of preference, which is necessary to the trustworthiness and reasonableness of preference in what we accept and reject.

AUTONOMY, CONCEPTUAL CHANGE, AND SCIENTIFIC REVOLUTION

The role of autonomy and the attachment of exemplar representation to our representation and description of the external world have serious philosophical consequences for issues of conceptual change in scientific thought and discourse. Note that the attachment of the exemplar representation of the offensive odor might have been attached by mistake to some other creature, perhaps a large rattlesnake passing by when the stink is experienced. As further experience and the testimony of knowledgeable others leads us to correct our mistake, we detach the exemplar representation from the snake and attach it to a skunk. This trivial example provides the basic understanding of the relation of experience to more radical conceptual shifts and scientific revolutions. Simply put, exemplar representations of experience may be attached, detached, and reattached to our conceptions and descriptions of the external world as part of the functional meaning and content of them. The exemplar representation in terms of the experience itself contains a reflexive reference of the exemplar of experience back onto itself. This reflexive reference provides an independence from the frameworks of conception and description of the objects of the external world. It allows us to semantically connect our description of the external objects with exemplar representation of experience in the language of thought. The semantic connection provides our description of the external world with a truth connection to experience.

Sellars, I argue in Chapter 5 and more fully in (2012b), saw the role of exemplars in semantic shifts from common-sense description of the world, the manifest image, to scientific description, the scientific image, maintaining a connection between the stimulus of sense experience and our varying conceptions of the world. Exemplar representations are attached, detached, and reattached in the shift from common-sense representation to scientific representation, and, moreover, from one scientific revolution to another. The exemplar representations of our experiences sustain an evidential connection to experience through scientific shifts, however radical, and without that sustenance the connection between science and experience would be lost. It might be objected that how we represent experience will itself be determined by our background theories. It must be admitted that our background system influences how we externalize from exemplar experience to a description of the external world. However, the reflexive representation of the exemplar back onto itself, exhibiting what it is like by being what it is like, retains an independence from our background theory. Reflexive representation might not seem like much security from error. However, aggregating this one-to-one correspondence of representation to truth in a diversity of individuals provides a social, scientific, and collective prophylactic against error that Page (2008) has proven to be effective.

MEANING, TRUTH AND EVIDENCE

I conclude by proposing a theory of meaning referred to in Chapter 3 that yields the connection to evidence and truth I have assumed. The theory is a functional role theory of the meaning of a word, articulating the use of the word in the idiolect of an individual and in the communal language.

Many details of a functional role theory of meaning will be complicated and controversial. Here I am only articulating some features of such a theory that I consider empirically confirmed. The theory was originally articulated by A. Lehrer and K. Lehrer (1995, 1998), following a suggestion by K. Lehrer and Wagner (1980). Two basic components of the theory, which I call *LL*, are conditions of the application of a word and semantic relations between words. These are treated as dispositions to apply the word and to relate it semantically to other words. We called the application conditions *reference* because a speaker refers by applying a word. We called semantic relations *sense* because those relations are what a speaker might use to convey the sense of the word.

How a speaker applies a word as well as how he relates a word to other words embodies indeterminacy. Quine (1960) insisted on this indeterminacy on philosophical grounds. This indeterminacy claim was treated as an empirical hypothesis and independently confirmed by the empirical studies of A. Lehrer (1970). In LL, we treated the indeterminacy in usage as probabilities, and the result is that the theory of the meaning of a word is stochastic, that is, probabilistic. The probabilities of how a person would apply the word and how a person would understand the relations to other words are in LL constitutive of the idiolect meaning of words of a speaker.

Moreover, on this account, the communal language is an idealized consensus of usage based on the aggregation of the probabilities of usage contained in the idiolects of individuals. The aggregation could be thought of as a weighted average that is a vector aggregation of probabilities that are normalized degrees of respect that individuals assign to the usage and authority of others. Thus, the communal meaning can reflect subject matter expertise delegated, as Reid (1863) and Putnam (1970) suggested, to those most expert in the use of words by the weight we assign to them. Reflexive exemplar representation provides reflexive security from error in ostensive exemplarization, and Page (2008) has shown that the aggregation of reflexive representation of a diverse collective provides a mathematical security from error resulting from the one-to-one security of individual exemplarization.

SPECULATIONS ABOUT TRUTH AND THOUGHT

I assume that how speakers apply a word is part of what determines the functional meaning of a word in a psychologically realistic theory of actual world meaning. I assume that the application of a word is stochastic. Meaning is stochastic, so if truth conditions are determined by meaning, truth is stochastic. This is a consequence of the assumptions that thoughts, as Horgan and Tienson (2002) proposed, are phenomenal states, that is, internal states that we experience. Thus, they are available to exemplarize. Suppose that Horgan and Tienson are right about the phenomenal character of thoughts. Then my thought that snow is white is a phenomenal state, that is, that there is something that the thought is like that we experience. We can exemplarize the phenomenal state, including the intentionality thereof, and obtain a reflexive representation that exhibits what the thought and the content of the thought is like, for example, that snow is white.

The thought that snow is white reflexively represents itself. Now consider the thought that it is true that snow is white. That might be a different thought. But if my reflexive representation of the thought that snow is white gives me knowledge of what the thought is like, then it may give me knowledge of what the truth of a thought is like. Assume that I know that it is true that snow is white if and only if snow is white. Then I may know what the thought of the truth is like because I know what the thought that the snow is white is like. I have exemplarized that thought. Now one might object that to know what the truth of a thought is like is still not to know what the fact that makes the thought true is like. But assume that I know that it is a fact that snow is white if and only if show is white. Then I may know what the thought of the fact is like because I know what the thought that snow is white is like. Moreover, the thought that something is true and the thought that something is a fact are both thoughts. The exemplarization of the phenomenology of those thoughts provides knowledge of what those thoughts themselves are like even without appeal to the equivalence assumptions mentioned.

A question remains. Is the phenomenology of the thoughts about truth and facts a complete account of truth, factuality and our knowledge of them? No! A complete account of truth, like a complete account of meaning, requires a functional account of the role of the vehicles of truth and factuality. That role must include an account of the relation of the representations, whether those of thought or discourse, to other representations and experiences. However, as I argue below, the relation of the representation to what it represents remains incomplete, and inadequate, without the exemplarization of phenomenology.

An exemplar of a thought about something being a fact has intentionality that includes factuality. The exemplarized thought is about factuality. The exemplarization of that thought includes factuality as an intentional constituent of the reflexive thought. A more complete theory of truth and factuality might decompose the exemplarized thought into exemplarized components. But that is not necessary to know what truth is like or what factuality is like. Reflexive exemplarization exhibits what the content of thoughts of truth and factuality are like. The experience of the thought includes exemplarization of the thought, and when it is about truth or factuality, those features are included in the exemplarization of the thought. The representation of truth and factuality becomes inferentially predicative exemplarization as the reflexive exemplarized thought is attached to the content of the thought affirmed to be true or factual.

EXEMPLARIZATION OF
TRUTH AND EVIDENCE

I argue that truth, though it can be exemplarized, cannot be defined beyond deflationary accounts as offered by Hill (2016) and criticized earlier by David (1994) which leaves, as Hill acknowledges, the informational relation between the vehicle and what is represented undefined. That condition of meaning or truth is exemplarized experience. Though the argument that truth cannot be defined by Heidelberger (1968) is overcome by Hill (2014), the informational relation remains primitive, and so it is relevant to ask about how we know what that relation is like to know what truth is like. To answer the question, let us return to the example of the exemplar representation of sensation as an exhibit of what truth is like. The sensation is exemplarized into a representation of itself that refers to itself and is true of itself. We know what the exemplarized sensation is like. We know what the representation of it is like. They are identical. The identity of the term of representation with what it represents provides us with an experience of what truth about the sensation is like. The exemplarization of the sensation provides us with knowledge of what the primitive informational relation involved in truth is like from the exemplarization of the object of truth, the sensation.

Note, however, that I am not claiming that the exemplarization of the sensation provides us with a complete account of truth. The complete account as Hill affirms is a functional account that includes the inferential connections of the vehicle of truth. A complete account of truth and meaning requires an account of the functional role of the vehicle of representation. But any description of that functional role of the representation will leave out something about what truth is like, what the informational relation of the representation to what it represents in experience is like. Knowledge of that relation is something that cannot be defined. It is something shown to us in the exemplar representation of the experience by itself, true of itself.

Having considered the role of exemplarization in an account of truth, let us turn to the epistemological issue of the evidence of truth. As I noted with Tolliver (Lehrer and Tolliver, 2014), Reid remarks that there does not seem to be any common nature to the various forms of evidence, the evidence of consciousness, the evidence of perception, the evidence of memory, the evidence of testimony, and the evidence of reasoning, which could be described. He adds that the nature of evidence is more easily felt than described. In Reid's words (1863), "What this evidence is, is more easily felt than described. Those who never reflected upon its nature, feel its influence in governing their belief" (328). This suggests that evidence, when we appeal to it in a specific instance, may be a feeling of truth, which is a felt quality of experience. To take an example, consider the evidence of memory. It is sometimes noted that the evidence of memory often fails to track the origin of what is remembered. I may not remember how I learned my telephone number, but I remember it, and what I remember has the evidence of memory. Of course, the evidence of memory is fallible, like all evidence, but Reid's observation is that it may be more readily felt that described. Evidence is something felt. Moreover, the psychological studies of Flavell on metacognition (1979) support the idea that the evidence, the feeling that accompanies the memory in the older child, is truthful. It is an indicator of the truthfulness of the memory thought.

How should we understand the feeling of evidence, and what is the role of this feeling in justification and knowledge? I note first of all that the feeling of evidence, like other feelings, may pass through the mind unnoticed. However, we have the capacity to attend to the feeling and use it as a premise in justification. The process of attending to a feeling and turning it into a premise involves the exemplarization of the feeling converting it to a predicate. We use the feeling of evidence we experience to represent something, in this case evidence itself. We may not be able to describe it further in words. We know what the feeling of evidence is like as the feeling, the experience, becomes an exemplar used to represent a kind of experience, the feeling of evidence. As we noted, the initial use of the exemplar may only be the reflexive use of the experience as a term referring to itself. But the reference of the exemplar radiates beyond itself to a kind of feeling, perhaps the feeling of memory evidence, and, more broadly, to the feeling of evidence in general. As in other cases, the truth connection between the exemplar and the referents thereof is something that cannot be fully described because of the role of the exemplar to exhibit what the referents are like. The role of the exemplar, not just the description of it, is part of the meaning or content of the exemplar representation. Part of what evidence is like, part of the truth about the evidence of truth, is something that cannot be fully described. This goes beyond Reid's remark about the difficulty of finding a common nature but may explain the difficulty. If what is common is a feeling, that feeling becoming an exemplar may like other feelings be something you have to experience to know what it is like.

The feeling of evidence has a bad reputation as people defend the most absurd views by appeal to feelings of confidence. This creates a problem for the justification of claims by appeal to feelings of confidence and certainty. My initial response is that not all feelings of confidence and certainty are feelings of evidence, though the former feelings are likely to be mistaken for the latter. The reason is that the feeling of evidence creates feelings of confidence and certainty in us. Though they are different feelings, they are all readily taken to be feelings of evidence. We know that distinction from our own case when we become confident of some view at one time and notice later that the view was not evident. The feeling of evidence is the feeling that some claim is evident.

It is crucial to notice that feeling of evidence of some claim does not exhaust the content of that claim, which is partly functional. The evidence felt is evidence for a claim that radiates and extends from a reflexively exemplarized state of thought or feeling to something external to the reflexively exemplarized state. As an example, I may have a clear and distinct memory seeing my old Prius with the bike rack attached to the rear of the car on a trailer hitch before I turned away from the car a moment ago. The evidence for the claim about my car may be the feeling of evidence that the memory is correct, the feeling of memory that I just saw the car. The feeling of evidence radiates and extends beyond itself to provide me with evidence of the external experience. It would be a mistake to think that the truth of the external claim was reducible to the thought of the Prius. The thought and the feeling of evidence may be internal states that I exemplarize. I know what the thought and feeling are like from the reflexive exemplarization of them. I know *something* about what the external objects are like from my exemplarized internal states. But the external objects and states of affairs, though represented by the internal exemplars, are distinct and separate from the exemplars that provide evidence for their external existence by representing them as we noted in Chapter 2. That representation and evidence supports our personal justification for what we accept to obtain knowledge.

The theory of personal justification I have advanced depends on the notion of it being more reasonable for a person to accept a target claim than objections to that claim. I have argued that the trustworthiness of the subject in pursuing the goals of reason in acceptance, preference, and reasoning explains the reasonableness of accepting one thing rather than another. If what a person accepts and his reasoning results in his preference for accepting the target claim over objections to it when he is trustworthy in pursing the goals of reason in forming this preference, then the preference is reasonable. If, moreover, he is reasonable to prefer accepting the target claim over objections to it, then it is more reasonable for him to accept the target claim than the objections to it.

What is the relation of the exemplars of evidence, the feelings of evidence, to this theory of justification? We have argued that exemplars of experience may come to have a functional role in the meaning of descriptors of objects, external as well as internal. They exhibit what the objects are like and become part of the application conditions of the meaning of those descriptors. I suggest that the feeling of evidence, the feeling that some claim is evident, may offer us some initial support for accepting what we do because of the evidential role of exemplars exhibiting what objects are like. The feeling of evidence may be a feeling of exemplars fulfilling their role of exhibiting what something is like. It may also be a feeling of our functioning in a trustworthy way in what we accept. The feeling of evidence may be a feeling of being worthy of our trust. We experience our trustworthiness in accepting what we feel is evident. The feeling of evidence is the internal sign of the truth connection.

EXEMPLARS, EMPIRICISM, AND KNOWLEDGE

Exemplars are the basis of empiricism in the theory of knowledge I presented at the beginning. Perceptions are justified by the exemplars of experience used to defend our claims about the external world. However, the background evaluation system provides the justification and the defensibility of the evidence of exemplar representation. You need a system to defend the exemplarized representation of your world. Exemplar representations are part of the meaning and truth conditions of some of what we accept as the target claims of knowledge. Exemplar representation provides some evidence of truth. Exemplar representation of sensations, of external objects, of thoughts, and of evidence itself, provides us with evidence for our target claims of knowledge. The exemplar representation provides an experiential connection for what we accept, sustaining the empiricism of defensible knowledge. The objection to our claims that they are only imaginative confabulations is met by the defense that those claims have the evidence of exemplar representations of experience. If there is objection to that defense, we have a reply in terms of our experience of evidence and the exemplar representation of it. Evidence, in this way, like the principle of trustworthiness, provides an explanation for itself. It is an explanation that is a defense of itself. But the defense must be free of error. We are fallible and have no guarantee that our trustworthiness and evidence of it in what we accept as the targets of knowledge does not depend on error.

We must be trustworthy for ourselves and others and not just accept that we are. Our evidence of truth must yield truth and not be itself erroneous. As I affirmed at the beginning, we obtain knowledge, and know that we do, only if our defense is sustained systematically in an ultrasystem that survives the correction of our errors. Our dependence on an ultrasystem for undefeated and irrefutable defensibility requires an empirical basis. This is provided by exemplar representation that allows for a diachronic and dynamic attachment, detachment, and re-attachment, of exemplar representation to how we represent our world, ourselves in the world, and our world in ourselves.

Proceeding in our scientific and philosophical pursuit of truth, we rest our case for truth on our autonomy in how we connect exemplars of experience with the meaning of our discourse. We must proceed with the humble recognition of our fallibility guided by the exemplar representations of experience that allow us the plasticity of representation and re-representation of experience to correct our errors. We have no guarantee of truth, but we have the capacity to dynamically change the content of how we represent our world as we exemplarize experience to correct our errors. The theory of knowledge as a theory of irrefutable defensibility succeeds when we exercise our autonomy in what we accept and how we represent the world to avoid refutation of our claims. We obtain undefeated and irrefutable defensibility by responding dynamically, altering the probabilities of experience, in response to the refutation of error. Sense is by sense corrected, as Hobbes ([1651] 1994) claimed, but only as the result of the exercise of our trustworthiness for ourselves and others in how we connect and reconnect experience with defensible systematic exemplar representation. When we succeed, we obtain knowledge that is undefeated justification and irrefutable defensibility.

5

INTUITION AND

COHERENCE IN THE

KEYSTONE LOOP

IN CONCLUSION, I TURN TO A summary of what I have argued concerning a traditional controversy in the theory of knowledge. I seek to combine history of philosophy with contemporary analysis. The traditional controversy is whether knowledge and justification are a matter of isolated intuition or coherence with a background system. Some famous intuitionists, Reid (1863) most notably, failed to acknowledge the controversy. He argued that knowledge was a matter of first principles, which drive intuition, but also claimed that the first principles depended on each other like links in a chain, as a coherentist might, and even added that there was one first principle that had a priority in the order of evidence. I have called it the *First First Principle* (Lehrer, 1998) that is evidence for the rest as for itself. Sellars, a famous coherentist, argued that all knowledge was explained by coherence with a background system, but, on the other hand, conceded that some knowledge claims were justified noninferentially, as an intuitionist might. This book suggests a resolution to the conflict. It is that there is a kind of knowledge, the kind that gives knowledge a role in what I, following a suggestion of Sellars (1963), called the *justification game* that requires of the subject of knowledge that he or she be able to defend the knowledge claim. This defense depends on coherence with a background system. I have called this *discursive knowledge* (Lehrer, 2000a) and now *defensible knowledge*.

There is a more primitive kind of knowledge explained by how experience functions in representation to yield truth. An experience becomes a sample or exemplar used to refer to and represent experiences, and, beyond them, the objects of perception and theory. I called the form of representation of experience exemplar representation in this book as I did earlier (Lehrer, 2011) or, more simply, exemplarization. There is a self-referential loop in both exemplarization, the basis of primitive or intuitive knowledge, and our theory of evidence, the basis of discursive and defensible knowledge. A keystone loop ties together exemplarization, yielding intuition, and our theory of evidence, yielding coherence.

INTUITION AND COHERENCE

The traditional controversy about the role of intuition and coherence in justification and knowledge is the following. Some have thought that intuition was itself a source of evidence. The character of intuition and coherence stand in need of clarification. Here is my own conception of intuition and coherence. Intuition is a source of evidence for what one accepts that is immediate and does not depend on other things one accepts, while coherence is a source of evidence for what one accepts that is mediated by and depends upon other things that one accepts. Put in this way, it seems that intuition implies that not all evidence depends on coherence, and the claim that evidence results from coherence implies that intuition is not a source of evidence. However, the matter stated in this way leaves open the possibility that the kind of evidence required for knowledge is a combination of intuition and coherence. It may be that intuition and coherence must be joined to yield the kind of evidence required for knowledge.

There is another way to put the matter in terms of the metaphors of the foundation and coherence theories of knowledge. Intuition as a source of evidence can be the basis of a foundation of knowledge because the foundation is based on intuition, a source of evidence that does not depend on other things one accepts. A coherence theory, by contrast, affirms that evidence for what one accepts always depends on other things one accepts. The standard objection to a foundation theory is that evidence, since it does not depend on anything else one accepts, cannot be explained in terms of what one accepts, and leaves us with an explanatory surd. The standard objection to the coherence theory is that it leaves us with a regress or circle of the evidence because the acceptance of something always depends on something else.

It is interesting to note historically that one famous foundationalist, Reid (1863), affirmed the role of intuition very avidly while at the same time affirming the dependence of the principles of intuition, which he called first principles, upon each other and, notably, on one special first principle which he says has a priority in the order of evidence over the others. Leaving aside a good deal of detail, he affirms the intuitive character of principles of our faculties. These faculties are original capacities of the mind that yield conceptions and convictions of consciousness, perception, and memory, among others. In each case, he says that the principles yield convictions about things that really do or did exist. So the principles appear to simply affirm the connection between conviction and reality without saying anything about evidence. But he holds that such principles are principles of evidence, for he affirms that evidence is the ground of belief, and first principles are the ground. What is more interesting is that he anticipates the objection to his first principles as a source of evidence, namely, that we are deceived and they are fallacious. His reply is the seventh principle in his first principles. I call it the First First Principle (Lehrer, 1998, 2010) because it is a first principle affirming that our faculties by which we distinguish truth from error are not fallacious. He remarks that this principle is a principle of evidence that has priority over the others, noting, of course, that our faculties must not be fallacious or else the claims on behalf of the other first principles of our faculties fall victim to the fallaciousness of our faculties. He compares the evidence of Principle Seven to light as we have noted earlier that reveals itself as it reveals the illuminated object. The First First Principle is a principle of our faculties, and, therefore, vouches for itself as it vouches for the other first principles of our faculties.

I think that this is more than a historical oddity in the philosophy of Reid. He is candid in noting that a foundationalist, someone who holds that intuition is a source of evidence, is assuming, whether he or she makes it explicit or not, that some convictions constitute immediate evidence. Without that assumption, how can one defend the claims of intuition and the foundational character of evidence? Put it another way, the foundationalist is assuming that some convictions have the evidence of intuition, and others do not. What is the source of the evidence of that assumption? Those defending intuition and foundation theories will usually claim that evidence of intuition does not depend on general assumptions in order to avoid the conclusion that the evidence of the foundation depends on such assumptions. But this is rather as though the intuitionist, having specified in general terms which convictions have the status of intuition, says, "Shh, we won't mention this."

NONINFERENTIAL EVIDENCE AND THE MYTH OF THE GIVEN

Reid was more candid. However, he left us with a puzzle about the nature of evidence that is as simple to state as it is puzzling to solve. Reid argued that first principles, and particular instances of them as well, both have immediate evidence and do not obtain their evidence from reasoning. Even more strongly, he argued that reasoning could add nothing to the evidence of them. The evidence is immediate and neither requires nor admits of appeal to reasoning for their evidence. Now this leaves us with a puzzle concerning the First First Principle. It is simply that the evidence of intuition, the evidence of first principles of our faculties, seems to depend on the First First Principle. Reid suggests that it has a priority, that it vouches for the other principles, and, in so doing, appears to provide a premise for reasoning in favor of the evidence of other principles from the First First Principle. Indeed, it seems, as Reid's analogy to light suggests, that the First First Principle explains the evidence of the other principles, to wit, that they are evidence because they are first principles of our faculties and, given the evidence of the First

First Principle, those faculties by which we distinguish truth from error are not fallacious.

Reid offers one answer to the question of why the first principles do not admit of reasoning in their favor, namely, that first principles have all the evidence they admit of, all that they can have, and, therefore, do not admit of an increase in their evidence as the result of reasoning. They come into the mind evident, as he puts it in another place; their evidence is their birthright. But why cannot we add to that evidence? His answer is that they have all the evidence of which they admit. What he means becomes clear when he remarks that the evidence they have is equal to that of an axiom of Euclid. The point is that there is a maximum degree of evidence that any conviction can have, and the first principles, as well as their particular instances, come into existence with that degree of evidence. You cannot add evidence to something that is maximally evident to begin with. So reasoning from the First First Principle could not increase the evidence of first principles and their instances because they are maximally evident prior to such reasoning. However, an objection remains. The First First Principle appears to explain why the other first principles are evident, and, thereby, explains why intuition is a source of evidence. The illuminated object would not be visible without light, after all, and the illumination of light reveals why it is visible. Evidence admits of explanation by reasoning from the First First Principle.

Oddly, a famous coherence theorist, Sellars (1963), who defended a coherence theory of knowledge, was equally candid in affirming that there were some beliefs whose evidence was noninferential. Sellars was famous for his rejection of the Myth of the Given, which sounds like a rejection of intuition. He argued that the mere existence of some sensory state could not entail knowledge of the existence of it. His argument was that language was required for a person to have any conception of the sensory state, and, therefore, for a belief that the state exists. The conclusion that the entailment did not hold was the simple consequence of the premise that the existence of a sensory state did not entail the existence of language. Not everyone was willing to grant the view that conception of something required the existence of language. However, the argument has a cogency that does not depend on the assumption about language being required for conception. The argument against the given requires only the premise that the existence of a sensory state, a pain as a salient example, does not entail that the person who has the state has a conception of it. Sensory stimuli are one thing, a conception of them another, and the first does not logically entail the second. Sometimes the argument is formulated in terms of representation rather than conception. It would use the premise that knowledge that a state exists requires some representation of the state that is not logically entailed by the existence of the state.

The reply of a Reidian intuitionist to this argument may grant that the evidence of intuition may presuppose conception and conviction, as Sellars avows. He may grant that the mere existence of the sensory state does not entail any conception or representation of the state. But he may argue that the conception and conviction that accompanies the sensory state, though not entailed by the existence of the state, has evidence that is noninferential. Reid and Sellars differed concerning the source of the explanation, but agreed that it was noninferential. Reid was a nativist who argued that the conception and belief arose, in the case of first principles, from the exercise of an original faculty, by which I suggest he meant an inborn capacity, while Sellars was a behaviorist who argued that conception and belief arose from stimulus-response conditioning. However, a conception and belief that arises from response to a stimulus, whether as the result of an innate faculty or stimulus-response conditioning could, in either case, be a response that was not inferred from anything else. It is tempting to think that any background principle, whether an innate principle or conditioned principle that explains the response is, therefore, a premise from which one reasons to arrive at the response of conception and conviction. That is a mistake. Moreover, neither the foundationalist Reid nor the coherentist Sellars made that mistake. They understood that inference from a principle is a causal process of a special sort, a kind of transition from one representational state to another, while other responses are transitions from states that are nonrepresentational, input states in contemporary vocabulary, to ones that are representational output states. Noninferential conception and belief is of the second variety. Not every transition from one state to another is an inference.

BACKGROUND SYSTEMS, EVIDENCE, AND KNOWLEDGE WITHOUT PROOF

Sellars was, however, adamant that the evidence of even noninferential conception and conviction depends on a background system. Though the noninferential conviction is not generated by inference from premises of the system, the evidence of the conviction, or as he would put it, the justification for the conviction, depends on the background system. Here is the basis of disagreement. Sellars thought that the background system serves the goal of maximizing explanation, and it plays a crucial role in what I called the *justification game* of evidence. Thus, the belief that arises noninferentially is justified according to Sellars because of the role it plays in the background system that explains why it should be accepted. So there is an initial contrast between Reid and Sellars that is characteristic of the contrast between intuitionist theories and coherence theories concerning evidence of noninferential or immediate conviction. Reid thought it was the way in which they originate that accounts for their evidence, the evidence of intuition, without appeal to a background system. He says they are born justified; their justification is their birthright of intuition. Sellars by contrast, though he might admit that how they came into existence enters into their justification, held that it is only because of a systematic explanation of why beliefs that come into existence in that way turn out to be true. For Reid, evidence of their truth is a birthright. For Sellars, evidence of their truth is explained by a system.

So who is right? Notice that Reid, like Sellars, holds that the first principles constitute a system. Reid says that they are joined like links in a chain and that you cannot have the links without the chain. His meaning is disputed, but I believe that it is the First First Principle that contains the answer to what he means. It tells us that all the first principles by which we distinguish truth from error are not fallacious. So if a person like Hume, Reid's target of criticism, accepts a first principle of consciousness but rejects a first principle of perception, he undermines his evidence for one by rejecting the second, for they are equally first principles of our faculties. By the First First Principle, they stand or fall together. Moreover, Reid says that no one will note his conviction of first principles, including the First First Principle, until they are challenged. So Reid, like Sellars, appears committed to the view that the First First Principle plays a systematic role in the justification game, that is, in answering challenges to evidence of truth, including intuition, for our convictions, including the noninferential ones.

We have reached an issue that is not merely a historical curiosity in the study of Reid and Sellars. Any foundationalist insisting on the role of intuition, whether Reid or his splendid twentieth-century follower, Chisholm (1966), confronts a question about the claim that some convictions have intuitive evidence of truth. Why do those beliefs and not others have this status? And if you answer the question by appeal to some principle, how do you avoid the problem that Reid faces in our account of him? Why is the principle that accounts for the intuitive evidence of the belief not a principle of evidence itself? And if it is a principle of evidence itself, why is the evidence of the alleged noninferential conviction not a premise from which the evidence of the belief is inferred? Harman (1973) suggested that all justification, all evidence, is inference to the best explanation. But even Sellars, to whom Harman is indebted, concedes that there are noninferentially justified beliefs. How can justification of all beliefs be explained when some beliefs are noninferentially justified?

The nature of the problem can be further illuminated when the intuitionist and the coherence theorist confront a skeptic about justification. How is either to answer the skeptic's challenge that we are not justified? If he appeals to something he accepts to justify the convictions, for example, Reid's First First Principle, or any other principle, he begs the question against the skeptic. Reid says that, when confronting the total skeptic, he puts his hand over his mouth in silence. Yet the First First Principle is a principle of evidence, he says, though he cannot prove this to the skeptic without begging the question. Reid does not take the path of his follower, Moore (1939), who simply insisted that he had a proof he did know what the theory of the skeptic implied he did not know. Reid's reason for not taking that path, and putting his hand over his mouth in silence instead, is the one often noted. To affirm that you know something to someone who denies all knowledge or to affirm that you are justified in believing something to someone who denies that anyone is justified in believing anything is to beg the question against the skeptic. So can we prove that the skeptic is wrong? If to prove he is wrong is to offer an argument such that he ought to accept the conclusion, we cannot prove that he is wrong. For to say that a person ought to accept a conclusion of an argument, when the conclusion is the very claim he rejects, is contrary to the rules of reason. So we cannot prove that the skeptic is wrong. Must we concede, therefore, that the skeptic is right and we are ignorant? No. We may know that the skeptic is wrong; we can know what we suppose we know, even though we cannot prove this to the skeptic.

PROOF VERSUS EXPLANATION

Moreover, the explanation for why we find ourselves in a situation in which we know something we cannot prove will provide us with an answer to the question of how the justification of all beliefs can be explained though some beliefs are noninferentially justified. The point, which is already implicit in what has been said above, is that what is justified by proof or inference must be distinguished from the explanation of why the belief is justified. A noninferential belief may be justified, as Reid avowed, because it is the First Principle of a faculty, or, as Sellars says, because of the role it plays in what we might call the *explanatory system*, without appeal to the principle being a premise in reasoning or inference by which we come to have the belief. The First First Principle, for example, is not a premise in the justification of beliefs that are first principles. Appeal to the First First Principle or the explanatory system in defense of the beliefs only arises when they are called into question. Moreover, when they are called into question, the explanation for why they are noninferentially justified may be supplied. A foundationalist like Reid and a coherence theorist like Sellars may agree that beliefs of this kind, that arise from clear and distinct perceptions of an object or quality, for example, have a security from error in the way they come into existence that provides evidence of their truth. Once we distinguish proof and inference from explanation and defense, we may, without claiming to prove that a challenged belief is true, explain why some beliefs come to exist in a way that makes their truth evident. Proof and explanation separate to exhibit how we know the total skeptic is wrong and how we know some things without proof or inference from anything else.

EXPLANATION AND TRUTH

There is an upshot and a remaining problem. The upshot is that our views about justification are not without explanation. Moreover, and here I side with Sellars against Reid, is that all our conceptions and convictions are subject to revision to improve the explanation. Note that explanation requires truth. If we offer an explanation from a false premise, we have explained nothing. Thus, the system that explains evidence and justification, even intuitive evidence of noninferential beliefs, must provide us with an explanation for why the evident beliefs are true. Moreover, the explanation, I propose, must include a defense of those beliefs against objections, for objections against the beliefs call into doubt either the truth of the beliefs or our reasons for thinking they are true.

So, as Quine (1969) argued, the overall system must contain a subsystem, a truth system, telling us when our beliefs are true, at least those we accept when we aim at obtaining truth and avoiding error in a trustworthy way. As I have argued elsewhere (Lehrer, 2011), if we aim at maximizing explanation, then the truth system that explains why other beliefs we accept are true, must, to complete the explanation, explain why it itself is true. Notice that the First First Principle, which explains why other first principles are not fallacious, explains at the same time why it is not fallacious, that is, why it itself is true. I have called such principles that both explain the truth of other principles and the truth of themselves *keystone principles*. For such principles that explain the truth of other principles, and thereby support the explanatory system, also require the support of the truth of the other beliefs or the system will collapse. I have argued against the metaphors of a foundation and a bootstrap in favor of the keystone. The truth system, or some principle thereof, loops back onto itself, which may suggest a bootstrap or a foundation, but those metaphors are misleading. Take the First First Principle as an example, or my formulation of a principle of trustworthiness, to wit, that we are trustworthy in what we accept to distinguish truth from error. Such a principle cannot pull itself up to the level of justification alone, nor can it serve as a foundation for the justification of itself and all the rest. For the principle itself depends on our trustworthiness in distinguishing truth from error in the other things we accept, in Reid's terms, on the first principles not being fallacious, or in Sellars terms, on the structure of systematic explanation, and with it the truth system. Otherwise, if we follow Reid's formulation, the First First Principle will collapse in the rubble of error. A false truth system in a system of explanation is a snare and delusion. It explains nothing.

Now it might seem as though the connection between truth and the explanatory system has become so tenuous no one should trust it. All justification, including the evidence of intuitive truth, depends on a background system whose truth system loops back onto itself. So how can we assure ourselves that our truth system is connected with experience and is not just a fanciful delusion? The first step is to distinguish the kind of knowledge that I have so far discussed, a kind of knowledge in which the capacity to distinguish between truth and error is an ingredient, as well as the capacity to reply to objections in the justification game to explain why one has arrived at truth, which I (Lehrer, 2000a) have called *discursive knowledge* and here *defensible knowledge*, from a simpler kind of knowledge. This simpler knowledge may be possessed by young children, in whom neither the capacity to distinguish truth from error is present, nor is the capacity to reply to objections to explain arriving at truth. I call (Lehrer, 2000a) this kind of knowledge *primitive knowledge*.

Sosa (2007) later distinguished animal knowledge from reflective knowledge, but that is a different distinction. Reflective knowledge is a kind that engages reflection, and though discursive knowledge may presuppose a capacity to reflect, in the activity of the justification game, for example, it does not presuppose the engagement of the activity of reflection. It is notable that Reid introduces his seventh principle, the First First Principle, after others, affirming simply that the objects of epistemic attitudes related to consciousness, perception, and memory really exist without any mention of truth or falsity. I think the reason, though this is speculation, is that Reid thought that young children were helplessly gullible to the reports of their faculties and to the testimony of others because they lacked the distinction between truth and error. So the seventh principle may find the place it does in the order to reflect the point that conception and conviction may exist in a person, in young children, and perhaps in animals (Reid remarks that they appear to have a kind of knowledge), who lack an understanding of the conception of truth and the ability to evaluate the truth of what they believe in the light of evidence. I would say that they have primitive knowledge but lack discursive knowledge, the outcome of the capacity to evaluate and play the justification game, even within oneself.

The question is what is primitive knowledge? I would like to suggest that it is based on a positive attitude, perhaps belief p, or perhaps having the impression that p. The attitude is not inferentially articulate, though it may imitate inference by association of the attitude toward p with other contents and ideas. Basically, I think that primitive knowledge is an automatic response to stimuli in the form of the output of representation, perhaps encapsulated as Fodor (1983) suggested, perhaps not, but not an attitude amenable to reflection on the distinction between truth and error. Resilient illusions of sense, the bent stick in water and the puddle of water on the sunbaked highway, are good examples. They are the conversion of sense to representation. Neither entailment nor logical necessity is involved in the conversion, for it is only the conversion of input by an innate internal program or principle to representation. Will this serve as an anchor to connect conception with truth in a way that insures that the truth system is anchored in experience? It is inadequate. The innate response system may be the result of processes, evolutionary tales of survival, that protect us from danger by overstating the danger we confront. Survival selection is not likely to lead us to a truth-refined response system. It may be better to think a beast is bigger and faster than he is to avoid getting eaten.

EXPERIENCE AND TRUTH

We need another way to get truth into the game of justification and even intuitive evidence to take us to truth. I have proposed an idea, one that Reid should have held but seems not to have adopted, though what he says leads in that direction. For Reid (1863) noted sometimes our conception of a sensation, a sensory experience, may be a capital part of our conception of some external quality, for example, in the case of smell. A conception of sensation, an odor, may lead us to a conception of a quality in the object that gives rise to the sensation, and, initially, that may be all there is to our conception of the quality. We have a conception of a quality in the external world, a stink, the example from Dante and the skunk, that gives rise to or occasions the sensation in us. This is his view of our initial conception of secondary qualities. However, since the conception of the quality is based on our conception of a sensation, the account implies that we have a conception of a sensation. How? According to Reid, from our consciousness of the sensation that occasions a conception of it. So the sensation gives rise to a conception of it, and, Reid says, the sensation itself is a capital part of the conception. Now this hypothesis reminds us of the view of Hume (1888) according to which the particular sensation becomes general by being used to stand for a class of sensations. That takes us to the proposal of Goodman (1968) according to which a particular, a sample, may be used to refer to a property that exemplifies it, for example, a color patch of paint.

I (Lehrer, 2011) have incorporated the view suggested by remarks of Reid, Hume, and Goodman about the use of an individual experience and the individual qualities thereof into a notion of exemplar representation. The experience is used as an exemplar to exhibit what it is like as well as the plurality of things, perhaps just experiences, perhaps something beyond experiences, that exemplar represents by exhibiting what the represented objects are like. Now an advantage of the account, not noticed by the other authors it seems, is that exemplar representation gives us a minimal truth security as the exemplar, which represents a plurality of objects by showing us what the represented objects are like, loops back onto itself as one of the objects represented. I advanced this view in the preceding chapter and briefly recapitulate it for the present discussion.

We may think of the exemplar as a term of representation, a sensation of pain representing pains of the kind it exhibits, for example, and thus true of sensations it is used to represent. But it is one of the sensations it represents, exhibiting what it is like as well as what they are like, and, therefore, the sensation true of other sensations is true of itself. The self-representational loop gives us some truth connection and security. Perhaps that is why we speak of knowing what the sensation is like, what kind of thing it is, as a result of simply experiencing it. We say, after all, that we experience the sensation, and, therefore, know what it is like. Exemplarizing the sensation gives rise to a conception, a representation of the sensation, as well as other things being used to exhibit what it represents. It is true of what it represents, including itself. True representation is not enough for discursive knowledge, for a person may lack the capacity to defend the representation, but it may suffice for primitive knowledge when affirmed by the mind.

A question for Sellars scholars is whether this argument is a rejection of Sellars's argument against the myth of the given. Have we converted the sensation into a representation of the sensation in such a way that having the sensation entails knowledge of what the sensation is like? The connection is not entailment. When one uses an exemplar in exemplarization to represent a class one adds, as a contingent matter of fact, a mental operation to the sensation. Some, Kriegel (2004), for example, hold that consciousness involves a representational loop of the sensation back onto itself as constitutive of the conscious sensation which may lead to the myth of the given. That view, though tempting, seems wrong. In an initial state of waking and other disordered forms of consciousness, the cognitive operations have not reacted yet, in spite of the presence of the sensation, showing us that exemplarizing, however automatic in some cases, adds a mental operation to a sensation, to a conscious experience. Exemplarization explains why having the sensation adds a representation of the state that is not available before the experience of it. You have to have a sensation in order to exemplarize it, in order to engage in exemplar representation, using it as a token of representation, but having the sensation does not entail that you exemplarize it or represent it in any other way. So exemplarization is consistent with Sellars's attack on the myth of the given. It allows us to explain how sensory experience can give rise to representation without entailing the existence of the representation. My conclusion is that a secure truth connection can result from a contingent operation on a sensation creating a truth loop of the sensation back onto itself, yielding primitive knowledge. This is the simplest form of exemplarization, ostensive exemplar representation.

EXEMPLARIZATION AND THE TRUTH LOOP

We are now in a position to understand how the keystone principles of the truth system are connected to experience. Exemplarization draws a truth loop into the truth system. There is a similarity in the way in which the exemplar loops back unto itself and disquotation in sentences like:

> RT. "Red is a color" is true in English if and only if red is a color.
> RM. "Red is a color" means in English that red is color.

They quote a sentence that is used to formulate a truth condition or a meaning condition. Sellars noted that the sentences use the unquoted second occurrence of "red is a color" to exhibit the role or meaning played by the quoted use of the sentences, in other words, to exhibit what sort of semantic entity they are. However, these sentences involve two tokens, different particulars, to exhibit the truth condition and the meaning condition. The relation affirmed between the two particulars is subject to the hazard of error that can arise in the formulation of any relation between two particulars. The exemplarization of a state avoids that hazard as it exhibits what the state itself is like. It is the particular state itself and not another particular that represents itself, and that is true of itself. To achieve this security, exemplarization is required, which differs from exemplification which brings in another entity, a property or a predicate. Reference to the other entity introduces all the possibilities of error that result from relating a property or predicate to another thing that is an instance of it. In the case of exemplarization, as Ismael (2007) noted followed by Tolliver and myself (Lehrer and Tolliver, 2011; Lehrer, 2011), the exemplarized exemplar is an instance of itself reflexively.

It is of some historical interest that both Sellars and Reid seem to have held views close to exemplarization, but did not embrace it, while Hume did so. Sellars held the interesting view that in discursive thought our description of mental states is best understood as a theory to explain the behavior of others in terms of postulated inner episodes which then acquires a reporting role as the terms of the theory are applied in the first person. As Stern and I (Lehrer and Stern, 2000; Lehrer, 2012b) have argued, it appears that Sellars when pressed in correspondence by Hector-Neri Castaneda to explain the reporting role, argued that there were physical states of a special kind, sensa, which we learn to use like elements in the disquoted sentences to exhibit what the inner episodes are like. His model, if we have understood him correctly, is that certain internal physical states have a special feature that allows us to use them by disquoting them to exhibit what kind of state they are. Papineau (2002) later held this view concerning conscious states much more explicitly.

Reid, though he was committed to the view that conscious states, sensations most explicitly, are signs of secondary qualities of objects serving as a "capital part" of our conception of them, failed to embrace the view that the sensations are representations of themselves, though he says that they occasion conceptions of themselves in consciousness. When I ask why he did not hold the view that sensations were exemplarized and, therefore, a reflexive sign of themselves, I can only conjecture that he thought a sign must signify something other than itself, or as he puts it otherwise, a sign must suggest the existence of something else.

Forgive me this historical diversion, but it may help to explain the special way that I am arguing that our truth system can incorporate experience into the stones of the keystone arch of truth and knowledge rather than leaving us with a mystery of how experience is related to representation. If experience is itself representational, if it represents itself as well as other things, we obtain, as a result, the truth connection within the truth system of representation without the need to explain how the representations of the system are related to what they represent. The exemplars are what they represent. Exemplarization closes the truth gap between representation and what is represented, at least in the reflexive case. Moreover, as we know what the sensation is like, we know as we exemplarize it, so we know that what the relation of representation is like in that case. The knowledge of what it is like may be in the first instance primitive. I am seeking in this essay and elsewhere to make it discursive.

THE ROLE OF EXEMPLARIZATION

I end with a caveat and qualification. I am not claiming that exemplarization is the historical or genetic starting point of our conception of the world. Actually, I am inclined to agree with Fodor (1983) that the starting point of representation is a form of representation that is automatic, perhaps encapsulated or at least protected from reflection, where we obtain a representation of world, the output of an input system, without knowing what the stimulus, the input, is like. Originally, at a very young age, the response to stimuli may be remotely analogous to the response of my computer to compression of the keys. However, we acquire the ability to reverse the direction of attention from what is represented to the input state evoking the representation. We thereby become conscious of such states and gain the capacity to exemplarize them. Once we have a representation of the input of our sensory experience from exemplarization, we have made a great cognitive leap. We are now in a position to evaluate the output of the input system, the representational meaning of the output, and revise it. Most simply, we can decide that the appearance of the bent stick in water, a representation of the output system, is erroneous and should be reinterpreted, re-represented. But that requires that we know what the appearance is like. We cannot reinterpret a term without knowing what it is like, even if we can unconsciously change how we react. So exemplarization is an ingredient in our cognitive autonomy. It gives us plasticity to change how we represent our world, ourselves, ourselves in our world, and our world in ourselves. The ongoing dynamic of semantic change, of revising our systematic view of the world including, therefore, our system of truth and evidence, aggregates vectors of exemplarized experience.

The background system, which I have called the *evaluation system*, is used to meet objections to how we represent the world in terms of our exemplarized experience of it and converts primitive knowledge of what representation is like into discursive and defensible knowledge. That is what I have attempted to do in this book. I conclude by drawing the account in this book into the keystone loop of discursive and defensible knowledge. I include intuitive evidence in the loop because exemplarization is immediate and reflexive, yielding a representation of evidence and truth. It is discursive and defensible because it explains how experience loops back into the truth system of the overall theory. Combining intuition and coherence widens the keystone loop that maximizes explanation. I invite you to modify it further in the justification game to increase our understanding of evidence, truth, and defensible knowledge. Welcome to the power of the loop.

EPILOGUE

A SHORT SUMMARY OF WHAT HAS been offered may be useful to tie my argument together. I have discussed knowledge, self-trust, autonomy, and consciousness. I appreciate the logical detail of the style of analytic philosophy. However, I attempted to construct a system for consideration. The risk of error is greater in the project, but my goal is philosophical explanation. As I observed the constructive and destructive work of detailed analysis, which I value and hopefully exhibited, I became convinced it takes an explanatory system, a theory, to solve philosophical problems, whatever the risk of error. A new theory of knowledge motivated me. Here are the components in brief of what I have done. The theory, suggested by my earlier work, is that there is a kind of knowledge that I have called a *coherence theory* of knowledge but now prefer to call a *defensibility theory* of knowledge. The basic assumption of such a theory is that knowledge requires the capacity to justify or defend the target claim of knowledge in terms of a background system. The defensibility is an internal capacity supplied by that system to meet objections to the target claim. The account of defense or justification both in terms of what is considered an objection and how it is met is initially an internal matter, though the influence of external criticism is essential to making the internal worthy of self-trust. It is a central feature of the personal and internal that it reflects the trustworthiness of a person in the pursuit of reason, most notably, in the goal to discern truth from error. I assume that a person may believe things prior to understanding the distinction between truth and error. Moreover, as many have argued, belief may arise before the use of reason and remain contrary to it. So, I took a different propositional attitude to form the background system, which I call *acceptance*. One has the freedom to decide whether to accept a claim or reject it. I formerly thought of the background system as simply a system of what a person accepts. Though acceptance remains the basic propositional attitude, the voice of reason within, meeting objections that arise from what a person accepts must include reasonings on acceptances and preferences concerning acceptances in the background system. I called the background system the *evaluation system*.

The role of preference is of special importance in the account of meeting objections. One way, though not the only way, of meeting an objection to a target claim is to reply to the objection that it is more reasonable to accept the target claim than the objection in terms of the evaluation system. What is the source of such reasonableness? The reply is twofold. First of all, the person prefers accepting the target claim to accepting the objection. Secondly, the person is reasonable in what they prefer. The reasonableness of acceptances, preferences, and reasoning depends on the reasonableness of the person, which in turns depends on the trustworthiness of the person in the pursuit of reason and truth. Trustworthiness does not guarantee success, for we are fallible, but the trustworthiness of a person is the source of the reasonableness in what the person accepts, prefers, and how they reason. Of course, the trustworthiness of a person, which amounts to being worthy of self-trust, is not a blank check but depends in turn on what a person accepts, prefers to accept, and how they reason. There is a loop of trustworthiness to the manifestations of it and back onto itself.

Given the fallibility of our trustworthiness in discerning truth from error, defensibility of justification in terms of an internal system is not sufficient for knowledge. An external truth constraint is required, namely, that the defense is not defeated or refuted by errors in the evaluation system that supplies the defense. Defense or justification that is not defeated or refuted by errors in the background system is defensible knowledge. I have called the subsystem of the evaluation system cleansed of error the *ultrasystem* of a person. That system tests personal defense and justification to yield the undefeated and irrefutable defense.

This account left us with two problems. One concerns truth. The question is whether the background system connects representation with experience and what we accept with empirical truth. The most fundamental change in my reflections on knowledge is that I argue that conscious experience can become a vehicle of representation as the experience is used to represent what it is like by exhibiting what it is like. Such experience is self-representational, and the acceptance of such a representation closes the gap between the vehicle of representation and the experience that makes it true. The truth-maker and the representation of it are one. Representation incorporates instantiation. The role of such self-representation or reflexive representation provides the empirical connection of representation with phenomenology and acceptance. The process, which I called *exemplarization*, must yield exemplar representation. When it does, however, there is an identity between the vehicle representation and the truth-maker. Moreover, as we know what the exemplarized experience is like, we know something about what truth is like as we experience the identity of representation and truth-maker.

What is the connection between reflexive exemplar representation and other representations? The exemplar representation may be attached to represent other experiences, as well as external qualities and external objects, exhibiting what it is like to experience them. Radiating and extending semantic connections, one might think of them as stochastic-meaning connections. The exemplarized experiences become exhibits of what the external entities are like, or at least, what it is like to experience them. In this way, the accepted premises of our experience, our exemplar representations, become part of the justification and defense of target knowledge claims within our evaluation system. Our reasonings from the evidence of premises of exemplarized experience to conclusions extending beyond them become part of that system. When objections are met and the defense of the target claim is undefeated and unrefuted by errors in our system, we obtain defensible knowledge. Notice the role of the evaluation system even in the defense of exemplar representation. The process of exemplarization must itself be trustworthy and be defended against the objection that it is not. The defense appeals to and depends on the evaluation system as the exemplar representation is included within it.

Some will think of exemplar representations of experience as foundations of our knowledge as they provide evidence, though use as evidence requires the system support of their trustworthiness. I have suggested the metaphor of a keystone in the arch of reason and argued before that the principle of trustworthiness is the keystone in the arch of acceptance. I amend the metaphor to include a pair of stones at the base of the arch that are exemplar representations of the internal and external world. They would sit useless on the ground of knowledge without the arch of acceptance and the keystone holding it together. I acknowledge, however, the special role of experience and the exemplar representation of it in an arch of empirical knowledge.

Exemplar representation can be attached to other representations. The attachment is stochastic, even if it is semantic and constitutive of meaning. This entails that what is attached can be detached. We all know this as we discover the illusions of sense. When an illusion is understood, moreover, the experience is detached from one representation and attached to another. Here we confront the connection between freedom and autonomy on one side and representation and acceptance on the other. We have autonomy in how we represent the world and what we accept about it. The dogmatic fixation of belief may conceal this autonomy and the connection between how we represent the world and ourselves in our world. This is a mistake we transcend more easily by distinguishing acceptance from belief and knowledge. The dynamic change and choice in how we represent the world and the diachronic character of the connection of experience with meaning create the stones in the keystone arch of knowledge. Experience and autonomy are the parents of creative thought and representation.

The appeal to autonomy raises questions I have sought to answer. Autonomy, I have argued, is conveyed by a power preference. A power preference loops back onto itself as one of the preferences concerning a target choice. The power preference achieves autonomy when the explanatory loop is primary. One might object that reason, guidance by reasoning, settles the matter of what to prefer, even what power preference to have. However, the preference for how to reason loops back onto itself in what I have called an *ultrapreference*. The *ultrapreference* is itself a power preference. A power preference of choice is autonomous when the explanatory loop is primary, that is, when you have that preference because you prefer to have it. Power preferences for how we choose, how we reason, and, yes, how we represent the world and ourselves are an expression of our autonomy. Are those preferences in turn influenced by how we represent the world? Yes. Which comes first, autonomy or representation in the life of reason? Neither. Welcome to the largest loop of reason. Answers to fundamental questions of knowledge, autonomy, and truth are tied up, down, and together in the explanatory loop. I hope that the chapters in this book draw you within it.

BIBLIOGRAPHY

Austin, J. L. *How to do Things with Words*. Edited by J. O. Urmson and Marina Sbisà. Oxford: Clarendon Press, 1962.

Ayer, A. J. *The Foundations of Empirical Knowledge*. New York: Macmillan, 1940.

Bender, John. *The Current State of the Coherence Theory: Critical Essays on the Epistemic Theories of Keith Lehrer and Laurence Bonjour*. Dordrecht: Kluwer, 1989.

Bogdan, Radu. *Keith Lehrer*. Dordrecht: Reidel, 1980.

Brandl, Johannes, Wolfgang Gombocz, and Christian Piller. *Metamind, Knowledge, and Coherence: Essays on the Philosophy of Keith Lehrer*. Amsterdam: Rodopi, 1991.

Chisholm, Roderick M. *Theory of Knowledge*. 3rd ed. Englewood Cliffs, NJ: Prentice Hall, 1989.

Danto, Arthur. "The Artworld." *Journal of Philosophy* 61 (1964): 571–584.

Danto, Arthur. *Embodied Meanings: Critical Essays and Aesthetic Meditations*. New York: Farrar Straus Giroux, 1994.

David, Marian. *Correspondence and Disquotation: An Essay on the Nature of Truth*. Oxford: Oxford University Press, 1994.

Dickie, George. *Art and the Aesthetic: An Institutional Analysis*. Ithaca, NY: Cornell University Press, 1974.

Dretske, Fred. *Knowledge and the Flow of Information*. Cambridge, MA: MIT Press, 1981.

Dretske, Fred. *Naturalizing the Mind*. Cambridge, MA: MIT Press, 1995.

Engel, Pascal. *Believing and Accepting*. Dordrecht: Springer, 2000.

Flavell, John H. "Metacognition and Cognitive Monitoring: A New Area of Cognitive-Developmental Inquiry." *American Psychologist* 34, no. 10: (1979): 906–911.

Fodor, Jerry. *The Modularity of Mind*. Cambridge, MA: MIT Press, 1983.

Foley, Richard. *Intellectual Trust in Ourselves and Others*. Cambridge: Cambridge University Press, 2001.

Frankfurt, Harry G. "Alternate Possibilities and Moral Responsibility." *Journal of Philosophy* 66 (1969): 828–839.

Fürst, Martina. "A Dualist Version of Phenomenal Concepts." In *Contemporary Dualism: A Defense*, edited by Andrea Lavazza and Howard Robinson, 112–135. New York: Routledge, 2014.

Fürst, Martina, and Guido Melchior. "The Philosophy of Keith Lehrer." In *Philosophical Studies* 161 (2012): 1–184.

Gettier, Edmund L. "Is Justified True Belief Knowledge?" *Analysis* 23 (1963): 121–123.

Goldman, Alvin. "What Is Justified Belief?" In *Justification and Knowledge*, edited by George Pappas and Marshall Swain, 1–23. Dordrecht: Reidel, 1979.

Goodman, Nelson. *Languages of Art: An Approach to a Theory of Symbols*. Indianapolis: Bobbs-Merrill, 1968.

Goodman, Nelson. *Ways of Worldmaking*. Indianapolis, IN: Hackett, 1978.

Harman, Gilbert. *Thought*. Princeton, NJ: Princeton University Press, 1973.

Heidelberger, Herbert. "The Indispensability of Truth." *American Philosophical Quarterly* 5 (1968): 212–217.

Hempel, Carl G. *Aspects of Scientific Explanation and other Essays in the Philosophy of Science*. New York: Free Press, 1965.

Hill, Christopher. "Deflationism: The Best thing Since Pizza and Quite Possibly Better." *Philosophical Studies* 173 (2016): 3169–3180.

Hill, Christopher. *Meaning, Mind and Knowledge*. Oxford: Oxford University Press, 2014.

Hilpinen, Risto. "Knowledge and Justification." *Ajatus* 33 (1971): 7–39.

Hobbes, Thomas. "Leviathan." In *Leviathan, with Selected Variants from the Latin Edition of 1668*, edited by E. Curley. 1651. Indianapolis, IN: Hackett, 1994.

Horgan, Terence, and John Tienson. "The Intentionality of Phenomenology and the Phenomenology of Intentionality." In *Philosophy of Mind: Classical and Contemporary Readings*, edited by David Chalmers, 520–532. New York: Oxford University Press, 2002.

Hume, David. *A Treatise of Human Nature*. Oxford: Clarendon Press, 1888.

Isenberg, Arnold. "Critical Communication." *Philosophical Review* 58 (1949): 330–344.

Ismael, Jenann. *The Situated Self*. Oxford: Oxford University Press, 2007.

Kim, Kihyeon. "The Defense Activation Theory of Epistemic Justification." PhD diss., University of Arizona, 1992.

Klein, Peter D. "Human Knowledge and the Infinite Regress of Reasons." *Philosophical Studies* 134 (2007): 1–17.

Klein, Peter D. "A Proposed Definition of Propositional Knowledge." *Journal of Philosophy* 67 (1971): 471–482.

Klein, Peter D. "Useful False Beliefs." In *New Essays in Epistemology*, edited by Q. Smith, 25–61. New York: Oxford University Press, 2008.

Kriegel, Uriah. "Moore's Paradox and the Structure of Conscious Belief." *Erkenntnis* 61 (2004): 99–121.

Lehrer, Adrienne. "Indeterminacy in Semantic Description." *Glossa* 4 (1970): 87–110.

Lehrer, Adrienne. *Wine and Conversation*. 2nd ed. New York: Oxford University Press, 2009. Appendix by Adrienne Lehrer and Keith Lehrer. "Vino, Vectors and Veritas," 259–275.

Lehrer, Adrienne, and Keith Lehrer. "Fields, Networks and Vectors." In *Grammar and Meaning*, edited by F. R. Palmer, 26–48. Cambridge: Cambridge University Press, 1995.

Lehrer, Adrienne, and Keith Lehrer. "Semantic Fields and Vectors of Meaning." In *Lexical Semantics, Cognition and Philosophy*, edited by B. Lewandowska-Tomaszczyk, 123–138. Lødz, Poland: Lødz University Press, 1998.

Lehrer, Keith. *Art, Self and Knowledge*. Oxford and New York: Oxford University Press, 2011.

Lehrer, Keith. "Cognition, Consensus and Consciousness: My Replies." *Philosophical Studies* 161, no. 1 (2012a): 163–184.

Lehrer, Keith. "Defeasible Reasoning and Representation: The Lesson of Gettier." In *Explaining Knowledge: New Essays on the Gettier Problem*, edited by Rodrigo Borges et al., 169–178. Oxford and New York: Oxford University Press, 2018.

Lehrer, Keith. "Discursive Knowledge." *Philosophy and Phenomenological Research* 60, no. 3 (2000a): 637–654.

Lehrer, Keith. "Freedom and the Power of Preference." In *Freedom and Determinism*, edited by Joseph Keim Campbell, Michael O'Rourke, and David Shier, 47–69. Cambridge, MA: MIT Press, 2004.

Lehrer, Keith. "Freedom of Preference: A Defense of Compatibilism." *The Journal of Ethics* 20 (2016): 35–46.

Lehrer, Keith. "Knowing Content in the Visual Arts." In *Knowing Art*, edited by Dominic Lopes and Matthew Kieran, 1–18. Dordrecht: Springer, 2006.

Lehrer, Keith. *Knowledge*. Oxford: Clarendon Press, 1974.

Lehrer, Keith. "Loop Theory: Knowledge, Art and Autonomy." *John Dewey Lecture, Proceedings and Addresses of the American Philosophical Association* 81, no. 2 (2007): 121–136.

Lehrer, Keith. "Reid, Hume and Common Sense." *Reid Studies* 2, no. 1 (1998): 15–26.

Lehrer, Keith. "Reid, the Moral Faculty and First Principles." In *Reid on Ethics*, edited by Sabine Roeser, 25–44. London: Blackwell, 2010.

Lehrer, Keith. *Self-Trust: A Study of Reason, Knowledge and Autonomy*. Clarendon Press, Oxford University Press, 1997.

Lehrer, Keith. *Theory of Knowledge*. Boulder, CO: Westview Press and London: Routledge, 1990.

Lehrer, Keith. *Theory of Knowledge*. 2nd ed. Boulder, CO: Westview Press, 2000b.

Lehrer, Keith. *Thomas Reid*. New York: Routledge, 1989.

Lehrer, Keith. "The Unity of the Manifest and Scientific Image by Self-Representation." *Humana Mente* 21 (2012b): 69–82.

Lehrer, Keith. "The Virtue of Knowledge." In *Virtue Epistemology*, edited by A. Fairweather and L. Zagzebski, 200–213. Oxford: Oxford University Press, 2001.

Lehrer, Keith, and Carl Wagner. *Rational Consensus in Science and Society*. Dordrecht: Reidel, 1981.

Lehrer, Keith, and David Stern. "The 'denouement' of 'Empiricism and the Philosophy of Mind.'" *History of Philosophy Quarterly* 17, no. 2 (2000): 201–216.

Lehrer, Keith, and Joseph Tolliver. "Truth and Tropes." In *Mind, Values and Metaphysics: Papers Dedicated to Kevin Mulligan*, Vol 1, edited by Anne Reboul, 109–117. Dordrecht and New York: Springer, 2014.

Lehrer, Keith, and Thomas Paxson, Jr. "Knowledge: Undefeated Justified True Belief." *The Journal of Philosophy* 66, no. 8 (1969): 225–237.

Leite, Adam. "On Justifying and Being Justified." *Philosophical Issues* 14 (2004): 219–253.

Lemos, Noah M. "Epistemic Priority and Coherence." In *The Current State of the Coherence Theory: Critical Essays on the Epistemic Theories of Keith Lehrer and Laurence Bonjour*, edited by John Bender, 178–187. Dordrecht: Kluwer, 1989.

Lewis, Clarence Irving. *An Analysis of Knowledge and Valuation*. La Salle, IL: Open Court, 1946.

Mattey, G. J. "Personal Coherence, Objectivity and Reliability." In *The Current State of the Coherence Theory: Critical Essays on the Epistemic Theories of Keith Lehrer and Laurence Bonjour*, edited by John Bender, 38–51. Dordrecht: Kluwer, 1989.

Moore, G. E. "Proof of an External World." *Proceedings of the British Academy* 25 (1939): 273–300.

Moser, Paul. "Lehrer's Coherentism and the Isolation Argument." In *The Current State of the Coherence Theory: Critical Essays on the Epistemic Theories of Keith Lehrer and Laurence Bonjour*, edited by John Bender, 29–37. Dordrecht: Kluwer, 1989.

Mosset, Olivier. *Pink Square*. 1970. https://www.wikiart.org/en/olivier-mosset/untitled-1970.

Neurath, Otto. *Philosophy Between Science and Politics.* Cambridge: Cambridge University Press, 2008.

Olsson, Erik. *The Epistemology of Keith Lehrer.* Dordrecht: Kluwer, 2003.

Page, Scott. *The Difference.* 2nd ed. Princeton, NJ: Princeton University Press, 2008.

Papineau, David. *Thinking about Consciousness.* Oxford: Oxford University Press, 2002.

Plantinga, Alvin. *Warrant and Proper Function.* Oxford: Oxford University Press, 1993.

Pollock, John. *Knowledge and Justification.* Princeton, NJ: Princeton University Press, 1974.

Putnam, Hilary. (1975) "The Meaning of 'Meaning.'" *Minnesota Studies in the Philosophy of Science* 7 (1975): 131–193.

Quine, Willard Van Orman. "Epistemology Naturalized." In *Ontology, Relativity and Other Essays.* New York, Columbia University Press, 1969.

Quine, Willard Van Orman. "Two Dogmas of Empiricism." *Philosophical Review* 60, no. 1 (1951): 20–43.

Quine, Willard Van Orman. *Word and Object.* Cambridge: MIT Press, 1960.

Reid, Thomas. *The Philosophical Works of Thomas Reid, D. D.* 6th ed. Edited by Sir W. Hamilton. Edinburgh: James Thin, 1863.

Reid, Thomas. *Thomas Reid's Inquiry and Essays.* 1785. Edited by Ronald Beanblossom and Keith Lehrer. Indianapolis, IN: Hackett, 1983.

Rorty, Richard. *The Linguistic Turn.* Chicago: University of Chicago Press, 1967.

Russell, Bertrand. "Knowledge by Acquaintance and Knowledge by Description." *Proceedings of the Aristotelian Society* Vol. XI (1910–1911): 108–128.

Schlick, Moritz. *Philosophical Papers*, Vol. 2. Edited by H. L. Mulder and B. F. van de Velde-Schlick. Dordrecht: D. Reidel, 1979.

Sellars, Wilfrid. "Empiricism and the Philosophy of Mind." In *Science, Perception and Reality*, 127–196. New York: Humanities Press, 1963a.

Sellars, Wilfrid. *Science, Perception and Reality.* New York: Humanities Press, 1963b.

Shope, Robert K. *The Analysis of Knowing*. Princeton, NJ: Princeton University Press, 1983.

Sosa, Ernest. *Knowledge in Perspective*. Cambridge: Cambridge University Press, 1991.

Sosa, Ernest. *Reflective Knowledge*. Oxford: Oxford University Press, 2009.

Sosa Ernest. *A Virtue Epistemology: Apt Belief and Reflective Knowledge*, Vol. 1. Oxford: Oxford University Press, 2007.

Stubenberg, Leopold. *Consciousness and Qualia*. Amsterdam and Philadelphia: John Benjamins, 1998.

Tierney, Hannah, and Nicholas D. Smith. "Keith Lehrer on the Basing Relation." *Philosophical Studies* 161, no. 1 (2012): 27–36.

Vautier, Ben. *Red is a Word*. Artwork. 1975. https://www.pinterest.com/pin/215469163392375135/.

Wittgenstein, Ludwig. *Tractatus Logico-Philosophicus*. 1922. Translated by C. K. Ogden. Mineola, NY: Dover, 1999.

Zagzebski, Linda. *Epistemic Authority: A Theory of Trust, Authority, and Autonomy in Belief*. Oxford: Oxford University Press, 2012.

Zagzebski, Linda. "The Inescapability of Gettier Problems." *Philosophical Quarterly* 44, no. 174 (1994): 65–73.

Ziff, Paul. *Understanding Understanding*. Ithaca, NY: Cornell University Press, 1972.

NAME INDEX

SUBJECT INDEX